THE RESUME WRITER'S HANDBOOK

Books available from
the HarperPaperbacks Reference Library

by Robert L. Chapman, Ph.D.
American Slang

by Harry Shaw
Spell It Right!
Punctuate It Right!
Errors in English and Ways to Correct Them

by Robert L. Zorn, Ph.D.
Speed Reading

by Kenneth Roman and Joel Raphaelson
Writing That Works

by Alfred Stuart Myers
Letters for All Occasions

by Michael Holley Smith
The Resume Writer's Handbook

by Andrew Swanfeldt
The Crossword Puzzle Dictionary

The Concise Roget's International Thesaurus, Fifth Edition

Revised Funk & Wagnalls Standard Dictionary

Michael Holley Smith

THE RESUME WRITER'S HANDBOOK

Second Edition

HarperPaperbacks
A Division of HarperCollinsPublishers

HarperPaperbacks   *A Division of* HarperCollins*Publishers*
    10 East 53rd Street, New York, N.Y. 10022

A trade paperback edition of this book was published in
1993 by HarperCollins*Publishers*.

First HarperPaperbacks printing: December 1994

Printed in the United States of America

HarperPaperbacks and colophon are trademarks of
HarperCollins*Publishers*

10 9 8 7 6 5 4 3

CONTENTS

CONTENTS

PART ONE

STRUCTURE AND STYLE

THE ESSENTIALS

Although the structure and style of resumes have been changing over the years, the essential elements continue to remain the same: work experience, formal education, and any other pertinent data. Regardless of how the resume appears in final form, the purpose of creating an effective one is still to help you get a good job by stimulating interest and paving the way for a personal interview.

I have written and designed thousands of resumes tailored to fit an endless array of individual needs and complex life stories. From my experience in the business world and my understanding of the *job-search process,* I know that the best resume is the one that is easiest to read. The shorter, the better.

There seems to be a lot of confusion about exactly what a resume can accomplish, so let me set the record straight. First of all, resumes do not get jobs. People do! And no one is hired just because a resume is impressive, fancy, or convincing. Second, a resume

THE BASIC ELEMENTS

Name & Address
|
Objective
|
Background Summary

Work Experience ———————— Formal Education

Related Data

Military Service ———————— Special Studies

Travel ———————— Languages

Awards ———————— Volunteer Work

Licenses ———————— Summer Jobs

Membership ———————— Interests

Skills ———————— Equipment

Personal Data

is only one of several tools used in a well-planned job-search strategy. You will also be able to make your case for securing the position and responsibilities you seek in letters and interviews. The resume is only the bait used to lure the reader into wanting to find out more about you and your qualifications.

The two primary factors that determine the *readability* and *sensibility* of a resume are:

Is the resume appealing in appearance?

Does it tell enough of the story?

In other words, the final resume should appear sensible and professional and tell an interesting story of your career development and changes in a logical, outline fashion without revealing every detail in a laborious manner.

Communicating the essential facts is a matter of combining three specific areas of information in a thoughtful and provoking format:

professional goal(s)

total work experience

education or special training

To build a convincing presentation for your being selected as a potential candidate is a process of showing that your experience and training, supplemented by your personal attributes and professional goals, add up to potential and noteworthy benefits to the company in need of qualified help.

The upward mobility in your career path is expressed in both structure of format and style of content. What you want to do is presented as what you *can* do, whether you have already done it or not. All your resume can accomplish for you is a reasonable claim founded upon your current store of skills and experience.

Even if you are changing fields instead of just moving to a new position or another employer, the technique for persuading a prospective employer to pay attention to you is the same: Here's what *I want to do* and here's what *I am doing* and what *I have done,* which is why I believe I am qualified. Bring me into your office, tell me more about your company and the position, and I'll know more about whether I can do the job.

It's that simple. The major obstacle that most resumes fail to hurdle is that they just don't make sense, either in the way they look or in the way they are written. The majority of resumes—and there are millions in daily circuit—do not present the relevant information clearly and concisely, and they generally are missing the vital spark that creates a strong first impression. When they look boring there's little chance they'll be read with much interest.

This book is designed to help you create the best resume within your means and resources. Of course, there is no such thing as a perfect resume. It is impossible to appeal to the individual likes and dislikes of all screeners, personnel managers, and other decision-making people whose initial impression of you will more than likely be from your resume.

I was trained to write under the wing of the late Ann H. Tanners, a veritable pioneer in resume writing. She opened the first professional resume writing office in mid-Manhattan in 1932, and her original concept still holds true: A resume should be inviting in appearance and tell the story, but not *all* of the story. Resumes were then, as they are now, a form of advertising. (BUY ME!) The trouble is that they have to attract attention while not demanding too much, which is one reason they have been trimmed, chopped, and compressed to the lean formats of today. The five-pagers of the 1950s are now the low-cal one- to two-pagers and snappy singles of the modern marketplace. No doubt someday they will be reduced to the size of a credit card:

SMITH/WRITE/20 YEARS/AVAILABLE NOW.

Reviewing the how-to-write-a-resume books of other authors on the shelves today, I noticed their tendency to oversimplify by providing standard formats to use according to job category: i.e., one format for sales reps or radio announcers, others for legal secretaries and computer operators. This seems to me an awkward approach to creating a customized resume, and I cannot see the value of this method.

My objective is to show you how to make your resume stand out in the crowd, not fit in. If you look at the statistics concerning the number of resumes sent in response to classified advertisements, you can see the futility of relying upon an average, mediocre resume. Sheer numbers alone condemn the bland resume to the "first file," the nearest trashcan, so why even bother if you don't go to the trouble to make yours noticed.

First impressions are not only important, they are critical! If the resume doesn't have the "right stuff" it's not going to be worth the effort and expense of sending it out.

The sheer numbers can work for you as well as against you. For example, if your resume is in a possible pile of several dozen, chances are that most of the other resumes will be cumbersome, sloppily typed, confusing, or even outright unrelated to the qualifications sought by the employer. Hence, your resume— designed properly, written properly—will stand out just by being sensible and easy to read.

I will say it over and over again in the pages of this book: A good cover letter is utterly crucial to the package. The more personable letter ("I think," "I am," "My achievements") embellishes the more objective resume ("Supervised," "Responsible for"). The symbiotic relationship is unique: The letter serves as a sort of witness, pointing to particular facets of the applicant's (your) qualifications and experience.

So, keep the resume simple. Dress it up a bit—a good suit, not a tuxedo. Keep it on track with the facts and add some color with the letter. Since resumes are not addressed to an individual, they should be readable to anyone whose hands they fall into. But the letter has a person's name on it, a not inconsequential effect because we all like to feel our correspondents have gone to the trouble to address us directly.

(Names can usually be obtained through some resourceful researching.)

A good letter and a solid resume produce results. You'll find your career planning worth every minute if you strive for the best communication.

THE OBJECTIVE

More and more in the swirling mix of messages and daily data, the resume—a lone and meager missive striving for a moment of notice—must flag down the racing reader. Whereas in the old days a declaration of a professional goal might have been omitted as a needless restriction imposed on the writer-applicant's possibilities, it is now an almost unavoidable necessity.

Stating your objective liberates the reader (more than likely someone you've never seen or spoken to) from the burden of trying to figure it out. A clear objective also becomes the passport to the proper channel. That means the first person who sees your resume knows exactly who in the company should read it.

Ideally, the career goal should be the result of careful self-analysis, career research/planning, and determination. It is not advisable to break down objectives into short- and long-term goals. In most cases, when an objective is stated, it should express a single goal or immediate direction.

A good objective may also have the advantage of highlighting your personality. Or it may flatter your prospective employer if you say you want to work with their "cutting-edge laboratory," "innovative marketing group," or "high-growth and profit-oriented sales team."

An objective, of course, is without value if it does not present your aim sensibly and without hyperbole. Don't insult your reader. Don't say your objective is a "responsible position" or a "chance to grow professionally." Come on! Who would put on their resume that they sought an "irresponsible position" or a "chance to get stuck in a dead-end job"?

Stating an objective of "management" or "people-oriented position" creates little focus. Try to be specific about what layer or level of management you are aiming for, or how you want to interact with other people on the team.

What if you have two or more different objectives? If you are looking for a job, for instance, in either technical sales or product research, make two different versions of your resume. That can be the same resume printed twice, once for each objective. (You can paste over "Technical Sales" with "Product Research," or you may want to slant your experience to support your different goals.) You can print five resume versions with five different objectives if you like; print them on different-colored paper so you can keep track of them. It can be worth the extra effort.

EXAMPLES OF OBJECTIVES

Administrative Assistant/Management Trainee seeking an opportunity to utilize academic studies in a part-time position while attending college.

Laboratory technician with six years of experience interested in a position as a Research Assistant. Available immediately.

Personnel Manager—Purchasing Agent
HOSPITAL ADMINISTRATION
Strong EEP/AAP & Salary
Administration Experience

Marketing Executive: Sales Promotions, Consumer Trends, Product Development, Customer Service, Market Identification.

Fashion Designer—Metropolitan
Manufacturer—Will Freelance

Building construction position (prefer supervisory) with a major commercial contractor in the Denver area.

PLANT MANAGER Able to handle own responsibilities and work as team member. Shirt-sleeve supervisor who doesn't mind getting his hands dirty to get a job done effectively and efficiently.

Real Estate Sales
COMMERCIAL & RESIDENTIAL

A position in human resources drawing upon experience in program planning, budget analysis, service evaluations, and cost-benefit studies and special reports.

SALES/MARKETING MANAGER
National/Regional

To direct contracted activities or to direct the allocation of resources and funds for continuing operations, special projects, or capital improvements.

TELECOMMUNICATIONS
Position commensurate with extensive experience in systems and account management and traffic analysis.

CLOTHING TECHNICIAN Fifteen Years— Pattern Making—Design—Quality Control Production Manager, U.S.A. & England

Seeking a career in EDP management with emphasis on Purchasing, MRP Logic Systems, Warehousing, and Shipping.

A position as MEETING PLANNER in which a full range of experience in conference coordination and hotel operations may be utilized. Able to relocate immediately.

PROPERTY MANAGER

Strong background in all aspects of residential and commercial property management, including: Budgeting and Forecasting, Leasing and Contract Negotiations, Purchasing and Billing, Expense Reports, and Profit Analysis.

To obtain a rewarding position where my background, education and abilities in the areas of Chemistry, Biochemistry, and Biology would be valuable.

FORMAL EDUCATION

Formal education is comprised of studies undertaken in an academically sanctioned program, such as at a university or community college. Always list academic studies in strict chronological order: doctoral, graduate, undergraduate. Indicate the dates of attendance and degrees/certificates awarded. If including your major field of study or grade point average will be useful to a potential employer, include them. Mention your GPA only if it represents a record of excellence. Students should indicate their anticipated date of graduation.

Don't include studies never completed or those that are irrelevant, such as photography courses taken as a hobby but unrelated to a sales objective. Describe programs if the scope or length is not obvious in the name. Seminars and workshops don't need dates.

CURRICULUM VITAE

The curriculum vitae is a particular format used for a scholarly position, such as college administrator, librarian, research historian, or scientist. [See example on page 134.] The educational data makes up the bulk of the resume, as most experience is generally related to academic endeavors. They often include a page of publications (written/cowritten or presented) and a list of professional/scholarly workshops and symposia the candidate participated in. "Curriculum Vitae" is always printed at the top, and boldface and italics are generally used to jazz up the credentials.

SPECIAL STUDIES

Highlight any special studies, such as advanced courses or honors programs, to strengthen the presentation of your potential. If the course's name does not sufficiently portray the special nature of the studies, describe the activity briefly. Dates may be used but sparingly, and limit your list to those studies most important to your overall qualifications.

EXAMPLES OF SPECIAL STUDIES

Courses in Spanish and Art History taken during the summer of 1985 at the University of the Americas in Mexico City.

Certificate of Completion, "Mechanical Drafting," 1986. Jackson Technical Institute (1200-Hour Course), Jackson, Miss.

Modern dance improvisation classes with Merce Cunningham, Alwin Nikolais/Murray Louis and Phyllis Lamhut, 1980–1986.

"Secret Clearance Investigation Procedures," U.S. Army, 1991. "Terrorist Profiles & Patterns," F.B.I., 1990 & 1991.

Graduate (top 10%) of Computer Honors Program (Mathematics Department), Browning Military Institute, 1992.

Postgraduate seminars in "Speech & Hearing Therapy for Aphasic & Severely Brain Damaged Adults," UCLA Continuing Education programs.

Courses in graphics generation for artists and scientists at Brookhollow Community College (evening division).

HONORS & AWARDS

Emphasize academic achievements with reasonable restraint and be prepared to validate your claims. The more recent, the more valuable. Use common sense when listing more than a few, as "Miss Wool" would detract from "Class of 1993 Valedictorian" or "Student Council Treasurer." Obligatory social committee roles and fraternal organizations would be considered extracurricular activities rather than honors.

EXAMPLES OF HONORS AND AWARDS

Graduated *magna cum laude* from Cornell University in 1992.

National Merit Examination Letter of Commendation
National Educational Development Test Award
Ohio Regents Scholarship (Four Years)

One of seven students chosen to participate in a special 8-week farm and animal management program in El Salvador (1990).

IBM "Youth & Computers" scholarship, 1991 & 1992.

Southwest Library Association Annual Grant for the Study of Early American Culture and Literature, 1985–1986.

Iowa Press Association's award for "Best Student Television Production" (1992) for "Abortion & the Right."

Chairman, University Community Relations Committee, 1992

MEMBERSHIPS & ACTIVITIES

Listing extracurricular activities and memberships is a subtle technique for profiling some of your personal attributes (that is, one sort of person goes for debate teams, another for sumo wrestling). It is also often a takeoff point for a skilled recruiter when digging into your interests, and the initial analysis of your succeeding as a new team member in the company. Leadership and participation are the key elements communicated here, so limit the list to activities that were central to your developing interests and career goal.

EXAMPLES OF MEMBERSHIPS & ACTIVITIES

Elected Officer, Business College Curriculum Council, 1991–1992.

Volunteer in Children's Youth Services, summers 1988–1991.
Recreation Instructor (weekends).

Intramurals: Basketball (Captain); Indoor Soccer; Volleyball.

Panel Speaker (1991) and Member (1992), Conference of Legal Rights and Civil Procedures, ACLU/Tulane University.

Active in Red Cross and Amnesty International.

Representative to state conventions of Afro-American Council (1990–1992).

Founder of the Kids in Art program, 1992.

Artist-in-residence, Baltimore Summer Arts program, 1990.

Member of UNIT, a fund-raising coalition of campus sororities contributing to the Fund for Africa (ongoing activity).

AN OVERVIEW OF EXPERIENCE

The jobs presented and detailed in the "Experience" or "Employment" category are ones that you were paid for, regardless of the duration or amount of money earned. To avoid cluttering "good" jobs with "bad" ones, put the best ones under "Employment" or "Work Experience" (even if part-time/temporary or freelance), and the others under "Other" or "Related Experience."

Edit job descriptions for clarity, accuracy, and space; the more recent the job, the more attention and space it deserves. However, if a position was held only for a short time (three months or less), describe it appropriately.

Delineate major day-to-day responsibilities without extraneous detail; separate primary functions from infrequent or special ones. Titles alone will often suffice for the job description—sales clerk, truck driver, receptionist—especially for brief mention of positions early in your career.

Stimulate interest in your background by painting a compelling picture of your role and the environment in which you worked: inside or outside, alone or as a member of a small or large organization, under pressure or not, on the telephone or face-to-face, focused on details or on long-range planning, close to the chief(s) or far, far away.

Illuminate not only what you did but how you were able to succeed. Stick to the positive. You can discuss the negative aspects of a job (if you absolutely insist) in a personal and private interview, after you have had the opportunity to "read" the interviewer and can decide what is better left unsaid.

If you are able to state the scope of your responsibilities succinctly, tell what you learned from the experience, and elicit the potential you offer as a result, you have accomplished all you can expect of a resume. Be tactful, to the point, truthful. Save some of the good stuff for the interviews.

COMPANY NAMES & ADDRESSES

A common question is whether to use the address of the company's home office or where the job actually was. Use the address where you worked. If the company changes names, use the new name, but mention any responsibility changes related to the change. If the company moved, give the city where it was when you were there. If you were relocated, include it in the job description as part of your overall job-related activities.

Include only city and state without street addresses

and zip codes. These can be provided elsewhere if needed. You can delete the state if the city is a major one. This helps keep the address lines short and, believe it or not, may have an effect on your resume's readability because every bit of white space helps. Spell out the company's name and note the acronym in parenthesis. Indicate the particular division or department if the company is large and complex.

CHRONOLOGY & DATES

Chronology is the order in which segments of time and data are presented. Last job first is the general rule and most practical method. You may want to juggle jobs around in an attempt to cope with a troublesome chronology—usually too many jobs—but chances are this will only create more confusion. Follow the standard operating procedure and you'll be sure not to lose your reader. The simplest technique is to use only years (1990–Present; 1988–1990) rather than months, or list the month only for when you started your current job or ended your most recent one.

What about those *dreadful gaps* in chronologies? Like rings around the collar, they symbolize some type of failing. At an interview you can explain them, but on the resume they look like periods of floundering and uncertainty, if not laziness. Actually, they could have been the better times of your life: the months in Europe, the year in Alaska, the summer on your uncle's farm. But you can't necessarily put that on your resume.

There are two ways to "de-gap" a resume: 1) run the years together no matter what month you joined/left an employer, or 2) assemble the flotsam and jetsam of your career changes under a single, all-encompassing time period. For example, instead of showing you worked from 1 November 1990 to 28 January 1991 (a mere three months), stretch it: 1990–1991. It looks better this way and you can explain it later.

Remember, on the resume, we're after the best first impression.

On the other hand, if in a three-year period you had a lot of different jobs, it might look better to list them without dates under the same heading (1989—Present). If you really get bogged down on dates, eliminate them. Push your skills and experience by playing up the titles and responsibilities; put the dates in the parenthetical closet. It's not so important when or for how long you did something. It's what you *did* and *can do* that's of value.

REASONS FOR LEAVING

Reasons for leaving rarely belong on the resume. Provide them on an application form or in an interview; wait until you are asked and then be tactful if not sublime. The usual reasons for leaving a job—better pay, moved, laid off—are best dealt with once you are confronted by an interviewer. (That goes for other reasons too: sexual harassment, outrageous schedule, bad pay, stupid boss, unhealthy workplace.) Candor and honesty must be offered in well-measured doses; the truth can backfire. The guiding principle is to avoid any negative comments regarding any employer, past or present.

There are occasionally exceptions to the rule, such as for indicating why you want to leave your present job. Although this information should probably be relayed in the cover letter, there are times when a career zigzags so much it becomes necessary to impose some control and order any way possible.

For instance, one of my clients left a career as a production supervisor for a manufacturer because he was laid off. For the next five years, through inflation and recession, he wandered aimlessly from one semi-promising job to another, ending up as a manager of a motel in a Texas boomtown. After a year of this he was ready—hungry!—to return to manufacturing at any level.

Although the times were better, so was the competition. We needed a good angle to make some sense out of his confused and scattered work history. The problem of the various jobs could be handled, but the last job of motel manager was a tough jump point to work with.

As we discussed his situation I learned that the motel had been owned by his father, a widower in ill health, who had asked for his son's help while he either regained his strength or got rid of the place. The story began to make sense and I saw our angle: stating the reason he took the job in the first place, thereby putting the facts in a positive and favorable light. Our case: He was ready to get back on his career path; he had been off course (in part) because he was helping his dad.

As usual, the best solution was the simplest one.

NAMES OF SUPERVISORS

They also hardly ever belong on resumes. Application forms are the appropriate place to list them, for what they're worth. Other people's names certainly shouldn't take up precious space on your resume, all of which should be utilized to advertise you.

There is an exception: If your boss or team leader is particularly well-known and respected and would likely be recognized by the people you're trying to reach, associating yourself with him or her on your resume couldn't hurt. Just make sure you have the person's permission first and can count on the person as a good and valid reference.

So much for names of supervisors, but titles you reported to is another matter. In many professions it is helpful to indicate the position to which you were responsible. If you report directly to the president, say so. If you were told you would be under the authority of the linear control engineer but actually were at the mercy of the space planner, say it like it really was. Give the title but not the name. [See resume on page 123.]

DOCUMENTATION

Watch out! Anticipate having to document any and every claim you make on the resume, especially with regard to proclaimed achievements in sales or profit production. Be reasonable. Better yet, give the gist—improved sales—but hold the numbers for later.

You may be asked to document training programs, sales totals, awards, and the like. Don't send your evidence along with the resume. Take your proof with you to the interview and have it at hand at the right time. Incidentally, make a habit of obtaining copies of awards and letters of recommendation as soon as possible. The longer you wait, the harder it gets.

CONFIDENTIALITY

Confidentiality is a concern only for the employed person who is looking around, but knows he or she could get caught in a trap if not cautious. It's no laughing matter if you're going to be fired or replaced because your boss knows you've got your mind on leaving. More than a few corporate scoundrels have stirred up trouble by running blind ads to see how many of their own staff are jumping ship and sneaking out the back door.

Here's the curious dilemma. First of all, the presently employed candidate is in a better position than the unemployed. For one thing, the presently employed probably have more financial security which so quickly fades away for the unemployed. And because employers seem to prefer to hire other employers' employees (for numerous reasons), the resume should stress this bargaining position. The problem is that if you put the name of the company on the resume with your name and title, the cat's out of the bag. If you cannot be completely certain that word is not going to get back to your boss through the grapevine, then you've got to find a way to fully protect yourself.

There are several standard solutions, depending upon the degree of confidentiality required. Interestingly enough, they not only attest to the confidentiality of the matter, but they have flags around your *employability.* They make you look like you're important whether you are or not.

TECHNIQUES

Write "CONFIDENTIAL" at the top of your resume. At the bottom write: "Please do not contact present employer until mutual interest has been established."

Write "STRICTLY CONFIDENTIAL" at the top and do not provide your employer's name; instead, describe in brief: "Fortune 500 Manufacturer," "Medium-size Oil & Gas Exploration Company," "Top Ten CPA Firm," "Major U.S. Rental Agency."

Use a pseudonym, give the name of the company, and describe your major achievements and/or responsibilities without stating your actual title. For the name/address heading use the form:

Thomas Smith
[pseudonym]
Post Office Box
City & State
(See resumes on pages 120 and 127.)

ON-THE-JOB TRAINING

On-the-job training (OJT) generally represents a formal program of supervised apprenticeship sponsored (and paid for) by a company for several purposes: to combine formal studies with hands-on experience, to produce measurable skills, and to provide the trainee an orientation of the company's policies and procedures.

It is presumed that upon your satisfactory completion of the program you will be assigned expanded responsibilities, hopefully with a new title and an improved salary.

Training not yet (or ever) completed should probably not be mentioned at all, as it might lead a prospective employer to suspect you of taking unfair advantage of an employer's time and efforts. Being part of the OJT contract makes you somewhat liable to "pay back" in time and production.

The following example demonstrates how effectively a good description of OJT can portray abilities and potential value. Both the formal coursework and practical assignments are presented as beneficial.

Moreover, in light of the applicant's career objective, the experience is notable because it shows that she is already accustomed to working closely with the type of people she hopes someday to supervise. And since employers hire personalities and team members as much as anything (if not more), this is a paramount point in her favor.

EXAMPLE OF OJT

JOB OBJECTIVE
Entry-level Production/Processing
Management

FORMAL COURSES
Communications I & II
Advanced Machining—Robotics
Robot Safety—Engineering Accounting
Systems Analysis—Heat Transfer
Polymer Processes
Fluid Mechanics—Vibrations
Strength of Materials—Statics—FORTRAN
Integral Calculus—Drafting
Machine Circuits & Designs
Machine Automation
Electronic Measurements

MAJOR OJT ASSIGNMENTS
[6 Weeks Each]

MAINTENANCE Locating and logging of all cranes and hoists at the Inland Plant. Recorded specs on log sheets and layouts prior to OSHA inspections.

PRODUCT DESIGN, STEERING WHEELS
Assisted engineers in locating wheels for testing by customers; chaired weekly team meetings; wrote update reports for a variety of projects.

PRODUCTION ENGINEERING, TITE-FLEX SPRINGS Assisted in preproduction start-up and set-up of a new product line: expedited, tested, and evaluated new machinery.

HOURLY PAYROLL Diversified tasks related to pay, deductions, dependents, retirement and pension requests, profit sharing, etc.

PRODUCTION CONTROL, INSTRUMENT PANELS Planned and scheduled materials for various production phases; maintained daily inventory and ordered materials using a CRT.

SPECIAL ASSIGNMENTS
Production Engineering

Weather Strips: supervised testing on production line, 100% inspection of parts, and control of production operating conditions for manufacturing difficult close-tolerance parts.

Brake Hoses (thesis subject): projects involved new processes, floor support, materials management, maintenance and replacement of new/old machinery, and aspects of production engineering such as cold forming, machining, and feeding parts.

ACHIEVEMENTS & MAJOR CONTRIBUTIONS

An achievement in this case represents a heightened level of performance on the job, an especially demanding task accomplished skillfully through determination. The success is measurable and recognized by those who should. Whether it was achieved solely as an individual or as a team member makes no difference, for it is results that count. Results are 99 percent bottom line related.

As far as the resume is concerned, a major contribution is something accomplished beyond the parameters of expectation, but not necessarily known or recognized by the employer. It may be a personal achievement no less significant than profit production or cost savings. For example:

ROUTINE RESPONSIBILITIES
Operations Director with responsibility for all warehousing and distribution (shipping/receiving), personnel administration, equip-

ment and fleet maintenance, budget control, and profit/loss analysis.

ACHIEVEMENTS

Created unit level incentive programs impacting 3,400 employees nationwide.
Initiated a standardized lighting program saving $275,000 last year.
Reshaped company's fleet insurance program that saved the division $300,000 (34%) in 1992.

MAJOR CONTRIBUTIONS

Rewrote regional branch personnel manuals and revised all executive screening procedures; published in-house newsletter and maintained effective public relations with community leaders; persuaded selected franchisees to participate in neighborhood Crime Watch programs.

EXAMPLES OF ACHIEVEMENTS

Streamlined corporate systems with significant annual savings: Telecommunications & Long Distance Services ($450,000); Distribution Written Orders ($125,000); Uniform Services ($85,000).

Planned, implemented, and directed a bid on a terminal building at a major international airport that was $25 per hour less than the competition. It required an informational picket line which was removed with a permanent injunction. This case was a classical "Boys' Market" injunction resulting in savings of more than $300,000–$400,000 over the next five years.

Created and directed an energy cost reduction program yielding potential annual savings of $2,000,000.

EXAMPLES OF MAJOR CONTRIBUTIONS

Developed computerized exception/trend graphic report that summarized monthly progress on mystery shopping program.

Performed in-house feasibility study for future expansion of firm to the Northeast U.S. territory. Developed more detailed staff charts and job descriptions prior to interviewing and hiring.

Initiated weekly scheduling of subcontractors to achieve delinquency reduction and maintain smooth flow of output during difficult transition period of new plant start-up.

Engineer in charge of designing a new Photomask Zero Defects Clean Room and converting a lab to an Ion Implant Clean Room.

Cut overhead by rerouting of assembly and transfer of personnel to critical weak-link points. Eliminated repetitions in warehousing/inventory; prepared detailed analyses of over- and under-stocked items.

Introduced five new products through innovative "Shop N Sell" point-of-sale promotions. Supervised creative production work.

Implemented a public relations program consisting of full-page newspaper ads, press releases, public service radio spots, bumper stickers, and door decal distribution.

Acquired excellent sites for microwave towers involving close work with numerous systems' representatives and extensive travel and field site analysis.

Developed Oklahoma as the second largest producer of group tour business after Texas within my region.

Positioned the Dallas office as the leading distributor of Gateway's 4-for-1 coupons of any worldwide sales office, domestic and international, since 1990.

Improved annual budget objectives by 5% and implemented new training program for potential managers and outside sales representatives.

Instrumental in decertifying union in warehouse operations; restaffed and remodeled district corporate offices.

Reduced $1.8M in discontinued inventory by 80% and improved original inventory plan of $5M by 14% while maintaining acceptable fill rates/cycle time.

Managed order processing of $3M golf glove business and consistently met inventory plan objectives.

SPECIAL ASSIGNMENTS

Work performed out of the ordinary realm of your basic responsibilities may be considered special assignments. There must be a qualitative difference between routine and special assignments. Be sure to spell out your role and the specific goals and results. By spotlighting such (successful) tasks, you show yourself to be of extra value to an organization.

If there were a number of special assignments over a lengthy period, they may be collected and presented together under a separate heading. Although you won't necessarily be expected to produce evidence for your claims, at least be ready to explain the special nature intelligently.

EXAMPLES

Assisted the owner in finding new businesses in the community to participate in financing and sponsoring summer jobs for 100 teenagers. Also secured jobs in cooperation with city agencies.

Supervised the construction of a processing and distillation plant in Costa Rica for 3 months; hired and managed 800 locals.

Assigned by commanding officer to plan, manage, and direct an operation of 100% air-transportable field surgical hospital with 144 enlisted personnel and $3.2M of sophisticated matériel.

Successfully identified breakdowns in communications structure for 6 separate entities; presented recommendations to the CEO; majority of concepts and plans for reorganization were accepted.

Designed new computer programs for interdepartmental uses: Data Room Background Security; Treasury Refinancing.

Interviewed college students for local newspaper's series concerning high school graduation requirements.

Between tour duties, served as investor for corporate funds and home office consultant to import distributor of French footwear.

In conjunction with the Data Processing Manager, directed the validation of new methods for troubleshooting of "tests-in-difficults." Recommended changes and additions to ICL-SW's testing procedures in order to provide the most reliable and economical test results to clients.

Reorganized Data Entry Department by changing personnel hours to match workload and the entering of results of finished work into the computer for smoother and faster reporting.

While maintaining position as office manager, set up and supervised A/R and A/P of four new operating companies, and maintained books and P/R for a fifth company. Oversaw conversion of old Burroughs system to an IBM System 34.

Assigned to special team to analyze and select a 200-line T/R Interconnect System with both WATS and Long Distance Control Service, producing $2,140,000 in annual sales the first year.

Chosen by the C.E.O., Iroquois Mills, to establish a full generalist Employee Relations Program to support sales management in the heavily organized five-state area of Illinois, Indiana, Michigan, Ohio, and Pennsylvania.

ACCOUNTS & PRODUCTS

Providing a brief list of products you sold or accounts you serviced helps the reader relate to the experience. It gives an idea of the places and environments (more important—the people) you're accustomed to working with regularly. A prospective employer may be interested in only one aspect of your experience, a particular account, geographical market, or product line. The key to getting the interview could be the list, but be careful not to give away any inside information.

EXAMPLES

Technical Sales
H.D. Maintenance & Product Finishes
Zinc Rich Primers—Epoxies
Acrylics—Urethanes

Leisure Wear & Casual Clothing
SEARS—MERVYN'S—LANE BRYANT—
EXECUTIVE WOMEN—KMART

Products: Adidas, Puma, Nike, Brooks, Tiger Tops, Spotbilt.
Market: Strip Center Off-Price & Discount Shopping Malls.
Territory: NM, CO, UT, NV, TX.

Major Clients—
Methodist Publishing Companies, Inc.
Christian Network Services
Baptist Educational Programs
National League of Synagogues

Called on major bottlers/brewers, glass manufacturers, and other industrial clients in Hong Kong, Singapore, and Bangkok. Sold SECO conveyor systems and KISTER rinsers/depalletizers.

National accounts, including Mr. Top's Goodburgers, Barking Bob's Banana Bars, Photon GamePlay Palaces.

FACTS & FIGURES

Think it over seriously! Before you corner yourself with any claims or pass out any privileged information, make sure what you say is not going to become a problem later. If all of the people who will see your resume are people you can count on, no problem. But if you aren't sure who will be seeing your resume, be careful. Always ask yourself: How could I verify this?

EXAMPLES

Sold an average of $18,000 per month of construction trade tools and equipment. Consistently 40% or more above quota.

Owner/operator of a bookkeeping service with annual sales volume of $70,000 from an average of 14–18 clients.

Supervised telemarketing operations and expanded staff from four to twelve, producing $300,000 in 18 months.

Took over "sinking" national accounts activity and became top troubleshooter for corporate services ($1.7M base). Retrained operators and redeveloped product packages to custom specs.

Developed and coordinated pilot training system for use in depressed markets. Initiated nationwide entertainment concept for restaurants and lodges, increasing sales by 35%.

Took control of unsuccessful marketing team and packaged repositioned product (with new price structure for dealers) resulting in sale of 600,000 units in 1992.

Produced $75,000 of new business revenues for advertising agency in previously unsought market: national professional associations and national meeting/convention planners.

Director of administration (2½ years) responsible for overall administrative duties with 300 company-owned restaurants, including picture board training concept and producing company's first video formal training program impacting 5,000 employees nationwide.

Founder and president: started with a $5,000 investment (1982) and built the business of home security systems to sales of

$15,000,000 (1992), employing 165 people in two states.

Manager, wine and cheese buyer: reduced store inventory 23% within first three months in position, and through remerchandising increased sales in first year 5% monthly.

Planned and implemented strategies at the division level resulting in $750,000 sales volume within first six months. Major accounts experience involving $500-million firms: computers/high-technology, oil, banking, hotels.

Spearheaded opening preparations for East Tower: 22,000 s.f. ballroom, 10,000 s.f. prefunction room, two exhibit halls totaling 45,000 s.f., an outdoor pavilion, and 10 other meeting rooms, including set-ups, exhibits, coordination of A/V requirements, staffing, and scheduling.

Rebuilt the lucrative Denver account base of a "Big Three" car rental agency from $10,000,000 to more than $28,000,000 in one year as the National Accounts Manager.

TITLES & JOB
DESCRIPTIONS

Work is what it's all about. On most resumes, a "good ratio" would probably be 75 percent work to 25 percent education (except for students). No matter how much work experience you have accumulated thus far, it's all you have to build on. Whether you're an artist or an auditor, we all face the same frustrating dichotomies of the job-search process: Either we don't have enough experience, we have the wrong kind, or we have too much.

Skillful display of titles and effectively written job descriptions can produce constructive results and perhaps even eliminate some of the aggravating rejection due to faulty presentation of your qualifications and potential. Remember, sloppy writing (and even sloppy typing) can wreck a resume. Job descriptions must be thought out and rendered sensible.

There are essentially two types of titles: the *actual* one on the company's personnel/payroll records and the *functional* one, which may be closer to the truth and a more accurate representation of your role and responsibilities. You can create your own functional title for the purposes of the resume. Also, noting the position to which you reported may add clarity.

Titles are the psychological handles we hold on to: senior accountant, executive vice president, editorial assistant, computer programmer, dogcatcher, shop foreman, shift manager, letter carrier, paralegal, tutor, mining engineer, fashion illustrator, contract coordinator, estimator, carpenter.

You can rely on titles to outline the various stages of your career, and certainly to emphasize any semblance of upward mobility. By *staircasing the chronology,* they can simplify the story.

1991–PRESENT—National Sales Manager
1990–1991—Regional Sales Manager, SE U.S.A.
1988–1990—Sales Representative, SE & NE U.S.A.
1991–1992—Comptroller—ADVO SYSTEMS DIVISION
1989–1991—District Operations Financial Administrator
1987–1989—Controller—CORPORATE SERVICES DIVISION
1986–1987—Manager, Tax Department (STATE AGENCY)
1982–1985—Accountant/Auditor—CPA Firms

Job descriptions must be whittled down to one to three informative paragraphs, depending upon the duration of the job. Responsibilities should be stacked in order of priorities, with the first entry outlining the parameters of routine responsibilities, and secondary functions or special achievements/major contributions listed next. Sum up your role and efforts without complicated details; tell just enough to stimulate interest and an interview. Use the telegraphic style shown in the following examples to get the point across clearly and quickly.

EXAMPLES

Senior System Engineer (8 Years). Maintain and install customer base with minimal debooking. Positive sales environment enabled Seattle district team to be at or near the top in total revenues. Responsibilities: customer consultation, system tailoring. Interactive and remote job entry communication protocols into mainframes (including BIM "SNA SDLC").

Field Service Engineer (6 Years). Repaired hardware on all remote terminals; used N.C.R. territory, Truth-Table system to service area previously requiring 4 men. Promoted 3 times. Responsible for overall administrative duties associated with 219 company-owned restaurants, including a nationwide remodel function, exterior signage, major equipment roll-outs, profit incentive programs, management information systems, and product planning.

Printer responsibilities: Perform initial analysis and respond to audible error codes; decollate, trim, and burst special forms; report abnormal mechanical occurrences to the customer engineer.

Tape responsibilities: Mounting to drives; swapping; reporting damage to tape librarian; intervening in threading breaks.

Purified High Density Lipoprotein (HDL) subfractions and cholesterol by column chromatography and electrofusing methods. Programmed research data into computers.

Contract Sales: Sold commercial and industrial appliances to manufacturers in Tennessee, Kentucky, and Ohio.

Service Center Supervisor: 18 employees in 3 departments (Credit Card, Parts Warehouse, Mail Order).

Purchased various items for all Member Bakers throughout the U.S.A. Products: commodities, sanitary supplies, uniforms.

Teacher and coach: curriculum planning and development; class instruction; coaching (four sports); assisting counselors and students in career guidance; recordkeeping; organized field trips to local businesses.

Designed a financial records system for comparison of budgeted-to-actual costs. Directed allocations and adjustments based on cost advantage analyses. Established one- and five-year advance action plans. Directed contract administration on 15–20 concurrent contracts; negotiated awards and modifications.

Aviation Safety and Standardization Officer at the installation level. Wrote regulations and directives for aviation operations; organized seminars; inspected flying units; PIC in Bell 205/206 helicopters for commanders and staff flights. Transported VIPs.

Design and development of military electronics for civilian subcontractor: 16-bit microprocessor circuit board with memory-mapped I/O and serial communications capabilities and on-board RAM and ROM; direct memory access circuit board using cycle stealing; EPROM and static RAM circuit board; MIL STD bus controller emulator and mother board with 10 circuit boards and 2 I/O connectors; integrated and debugged system using TI 990 and 9989, Zilog Z80, Intel 8080/8085.

Counseled ATM's top management and operating divisions on the United States and Missouri antitrust laws as they affected

ATM's operations and marketing activities. Also, analyzed prospective acquisitions.

Primary: Monitor cost and amount of usage monthly of electricity, waters (city and I), and exotic gases (hydrogen, nitrogen, liquid oxygen, forming gas, circulating water, compressed air).

Secondary: Computerized computations of "Plus or Minus" comparisons. Facilities planning for 35 departments in a 1,110,000 s.f. plant.

Began as Internal Auditor Trainee in a management training program and progressed to Special Assistant to the Auditor.

Performed routine functional and operational audits; reviewed company contracts with outside vendors; investigated fraudulent employee actions and defalcations.

Supervised shop operations: personnel/ work flow scheduling; wrote requisitions for supplies and materials; ordered tools and machines needed for special jobs; prepared weekly evaluation reports for supervisor; maintained budget; trained new employees; records maintenance and annual inventory.

Gardé Manager, Banquets: Catering Arrangements & Important Details of Planning.

Cuisines: French, Mexican, Southwestern Nouvelle, Japanese, German, Italian, American.

Prior Experience: Line Cook—Garnishes, Hot Relishes, Sauces, Soups. Formal Plate Service. Sauté Station. Broiler & Steamer & Fryalator. Mesquite Smoked.

Founder and president of a nonprofit "forum and clearing-house" for sharing and exchanging information and ideas to foster Christian principles affecting Americans now and in the future.

Administrative responsibilities encompassed all facets of fund raising and financial management, the delegation of funds, seminar and convention planning and organizing, design and production of media materials, and working closely with political leaders, the clergy, and concerned citizens across the state.

Beyond the scope of fiscal and administrative responsibilities, managing director, in charge of the Land and Title departments. (Company has five producing wells, one presently drilling.)

Property manager for 400+ commercial and residential properties, including 22 apartment complexes on the 130-acre "City Living Space."

Paralegal responsibilities: Liaison to City and State officials and all City Court and Urban Rehabilitation board hearings. Handled all Neighborhood Services citations: lost only 6 of 105 for a total of $17,200 in judgments. Negotiated commercial leases and demolition contracts, bids, and proposals for formal evictions.

Conference coordinator/liaison between meeting planners and hotel staff to assure proper set-up of meetings, exhibits, and meal/coffee break functions. Oversee the maintaining, set-up, and cleaning of all meeting rooms and the new ballroom.

Supervise 50 people in Housekeeping. Responsible for running smooth operations during the hotel's major expansion from 900 to 1,445 rooms, 24 to 58 meeting rooms, and a 160% increase in staff.

Evaluated stock levels for OTB; provided data for file building; evaluated product and sales viability; vendor/supplier analysis (2800 stock items). In addition, worked closely with upper management in special problem solving.

Responsible for the proper and accurate processing of loans: obtained information from applicants; verified credit histories; prepared and updated files on computer; worked in association with the Underwriting Department on special projects; initiated/maintained oral/written communications with clients.

Total responsibility for 9 customer service account executives and all aspects of personnel management and staffing; interfaced with all internal departments in facilitating client promotions.

Developed branch deadlines and guidelines to create client satisfaction; trained new sales reps and held weekly departmental meetings; projected sales volume per quarter.

Developed and implemented a counseling and recreation program for socioeconomically disadvantaged girls, ages 6–14 years. Supervised an outreach program at several low-income housing projects. Additionally responsible for networking with numerous other social agencies.

Routine responsibilities included the mechanical design, production, and shop fabrication drawings of skylight systems for residential, commercial, and industrial buildings. Other responsibilities: plant supervision in absence of the manager and materials distribution management.

Complete charge of managing company's lease vehicle service for field representatives. Maintained all financial logs and supervised daily posting. Coordinated requests for capital expenditures; acquired temporary staff help.

Organized a U.S.-based jean company (joint venture with a Hong Kong manufacturer) and managed all facets of import operations, including designing, producing, and marketing an extensive jeanswear line under its own labels: Pretty Polly (junior misses), California Cruiser (junior men's), and Darling Dorothy (full-size women's). Set up private label programs on letters of credit.

Direct line responsibility for coordinating efficient operations of home office and 18 branch centers: reviewed company and franchise locations to guarantee adherence to corporate policies and procedures. Recommended and implemented actions for variances.

Represented company at grievance hearings concerning the company's plans to remove rental houses and build a new parking lot.

RELATED & OTHER
EXPERIENCE

If you reach a point where you've got your major
work experience itemized under employment, but you
have additional background material you want to introduce, "related/other experience" serves as a con-
venient catchall. This heading may incorporate a
variety of work experiences (part-time, summers,
freelance) or foreign travel/studies, seasonal jobs, or
even activities such as volunteer or community work.

The experiences may be "related" to your job objective, e.g., selling encyclopedias door-to-door or assisting the manager of a seaside resort, or they may be
"other," i.e., not specifically related to the skills required for the position you seek. My feeling is that any
productive experience can be noted if you want it to.
It's your resume!

Because skills arise from a diversity of learning experiences, your overall employability is enhanced by
any particularly interesting things you've done: travel-
ing throughout Mexico on buses, stringing a pipeline

in the oil fields, singing in a church choir. It doesn't matter whether the experience was in a warehouse or a penthouse if it taught you how to do something of value.

The psychological angle is the important one. For instance, earning extra income during college as a tutor or window washer demonstrates your resourcefulness and reliability, and shows you are willing to take on responsibilities. To an employer, any work or educational experiences you have had are worth something.

EXAMPLES OF RELATED EXPERIENCE

Organized a senior citizens' Neighbor Health-Help program and ran garage sales to raise funds for local beautification projects. Active in YMCA and the Boy Scouts.

Spanish tutor and governess in Belize for one year. Art student and life drawing model in Mexico for two years.

Salesperson and cashier during Christmas holidays at Sakowitz and Lord & Taylor. Summer jobs: camp counselor; janitor.

Active in Big Sisters program and editor of church newsletter. Volunteer with Pink Ladies at Presbyterian Hospital.

Designed and built a "safe playground" for preschool children. Worked as a framing carpenter and carpet installer (1991).

Apprentice to the master lithographer Jose Guadiana. Studied poetry with Robert Creeley in New Mexico. Built geodesic domes in Alaska. Traveled throughout Europe.

Part-time jobs during college: school bus driver; survey crew assistant; waiter; gas station manager; cashier and courier.

Sold used cars in family-owned business. Snack truck packer.

SUMMER & PART-TIME
JOBS

Summer and part-time jobs may be included under
"Summer Employment," "Other Experience,"
"Work While Attending School," or even "Biodata."
However, if possible, experience gained in longer-
term jobs should be given greater emphasis.

College students must make the most of all the jobs
they have had because any work experience can embellish the academic qualifications, and such experience may be of interest to a recruiter. Just because you
haven't had much time to get a lot of experience
doesn't mean you should underestimate the value of
the jobs you've had.

I have talked to many graduating students who
were convinced that the summer jobs—lifeguard or
grocery stocker, for example—were not worth men-
tioning. I disagree. Think of how much children and
parents rely on a lifeguard! That's real responsibility.
And so is stocking shelves, digging ditches, counting
boxes, and the other myriad jobs we've all had in our
youth. It has to start somewhere.

People being busy doing something useful and rewarding are what prospective employers are searching for. Be proud of what you've accomplished, what you've done to broaden your view of how the world works. Underscore your ability to follow instructions and be part of a team.

EXAMPLES OF SUMMER JOBS

Earned 75% of college expenses as a typist/clerk, warehouse worker, cashier, waiter, and census data collector.

Summers: worked in a printing company learning how to strip negatives, burn plates, operate trimmer, and clean an offset press between color runs. Some cut and paste-up skills.

City of New Orleans Recreation Department, summers 1989–1992. Pool Manager (1992) and Assistant Manager (1991). Activities Director for Whitestone Park (1990).

Chicago Credit Corporation (part-time and summers). Data entry operator: entered, updated, and edited credit information of consumers; coded and proofread data. Xerox 820.

Sun Mart Confectionery. Hired as a general office clerk and later promoted to assistant manager. In charge of store: buying/selling, advertising, cash deposits, special promotions, banking.

Employment while attending college included: researcher for a state social services agency; office assistant and typist (law firm); secretary/receptionist (public relations firm); salesman.

Worked as a management trainee during senior year at Sportsman Package Stores while carrying a full course load. Duties included cashiering, daily deposits, ordering stock.

FAMILY BUSINESSES & SELF-EMPLOYMENT

Working for a family business is basically the same as working for anyone, maybe better at times (when you want an extended holiday) or worse at others (when you want more money). You do the work, you get paid; you don't, you get in trouble. You can assume that most prospective employers reading your resume will figure you've had all you want or can take, otherwise you wouldn't be looking for another job.

Develop titles and job descriptions to represent the level you occupied in the organizational structure. Aim the job objective and position descriptions toward the level you're shooting for. Simplify. Instead of saying V.P. of Sales & Treasurer & Office Manager, say General Manager. Describe the size and type of business operation regardless of the outcome. Beware of exaggerated salary claims! Many employers will just assume you're lying.

Like marriage, self-employment is one of those things that if you haven't done it you don't really know what it's like. The "stigma" of working for yourself is that others may think you are irresponsible (or a deadbeat), that you can't deal with the routine regimen of a "regular job."

To dispel that notion and establish your credibility it is imperative to show how you took on *more than the usual* responsibilities by being in charge completely. Show that your practical know-how is richer as a result. The failure/success of the endeavor is not an issue. Convince the prospective employer that you are ready to give the same amount of effort.

EXAMPLES

As office manager and controller of family's manufacturing company for ten years, held primary responsibility for customer relations, accounts payable and receivable, supplies and inventory, personnel supervision, deposits and banking, payroll, and bookkeeping.

Freelance law firm consultant and administrator (1988–1992) with experience in: Financial Management, Lease Negotiations, Office Design and Layout, Lawyer Recruiting, Office Systems and Technology, Policy Manuals and Procedures, Job Descriptions and Evaluations, Insurance Plans, and Salary Administration.

Self-employed conversion specialist (1991–present) assisting client companies with oil and gas accounting computer conversions: analyze division orders, oil/gas mineral leases, royalty checks, mineral deeds, and 6248s. Travel 88%.

Clients: Petroleum Data Service (Houston); Southern Union Oil & Gas (Oklahoma City); Consolidated Minerals (Dallas).

Purchasing Agent, Practical Pen Company (family business). Note: Took position at a time when former purchasing agent was unavailable for training and orientation.

Successfully mastered MRP system and improved order completion from 78% to 95% within three months. Negotiated with vendors/suppliers for 1,200 stock items, and provided data for new file building on DEC General System DS357.

Fashion illustrations and window displays for Brighton Beach Stores, Figure Eights, Moonlighters, Brown Derby Boutique, Annual JazzFests, Cisco Kid Amusements Inc.

Worked weekends and some evenings as apprentice to the printer in family-owned publishing company. Learned how to operate and clean presses between runs; some experience in photography and negative room. Adept at measuring for photo reductions and marking for halftones and captions.

Involved in father's trucking business for five consecutive summers: truck maintenance and parts purchasing; route planning and scheduling; special order arrangements; driving and loading; invoice problem solving and customer service.

MILITARY SERVICE

Full-fledged military careers of 20 years or more need to be "civilianized" to relate skills and experience to the open marketplace. The best way to do this is to break down an extensive background into separate functional areas comparable to similar civilian responsibilities. Here are the standard functional areas which may be itemized:

Financial Administration

Personnel & Purchasing

Planning & Coordinating

Office Management

Warehouse & Inventory Control

Contract Administration

Security & Information Management

Public Relations & Recruiting

Training & Evaluating

Maintenance & Troubleshooting

Data Processing

It is essential that you know where you are aiming the resume when developing the material. Career planning is the foundation for building a sturdy and persuasive resume. If office management is your objective, the data presented on the resume should be geared toward that goal, and extraneous data deleted so it won't detract from the more relevant information and qualifications.

If possible, provide some specific figures to demonstrate the level and scope of your responsibilities, such as "controlled $1,500,000 of heavy-duty construction equipment" or "responsible for training, evaluating, and assigning work of 300+ technical personnel."

Highly technical positions, such as in electronics, engineering, or maintenance, require job descriptions that indicate the type of equipment you worked with and the particular functions for which you were trained. Indicate any special assignments or performance commendations. (See resumes on pages 143–149.)

You may also want to make two or more different resumes for different vocational targets. In the following example, the first page (of a two-page resume) provides a technique for stating alternative objectives. Unless you desire to slant the second page's content toward different goals, it would remain the same for all three objectives.

FIRST PAGE—OBJECTIVE #1

Hospital Administrator

Highly qualified Hospital Administrator with more than six years experience in all aspects of administrative support services.

Professional background as a Lieutenant in the U.S. Navy includes budget preparation and administration, personnel supervision, records maintenance, and special studies. Especially qualified in analyzing and resolving organizational and staffing problems.

Primary interest is to join a progressive, growth-oriented health care organization and to contribute to its profitable success and expansion.

FIRST PAGE—OBJECTIVE #2

Administrator

Administrator with a high performance background in all facets of facilities and staff administration.

As a commanding officer in the U.S. Navy, experience has encompassed staffing and productivity studies, computerized information management, and financial administration at many levels requiring both written and oral reports.

Adept in visualizing the scope and impact of programs as well as synthesizing complex data for integration into current and future action plans.

Excellent coordinator who is able to track progress and control logistical details. Skilled organizer able to create and direct effective teams.

FIRST PAGE—OBJECTIVE #3

Consultant
Major Medical Programs

United States Navy hospital administrator interested in applying six years of in-depth experience and professional expertise as a consultant to major medical programs.

Primary qualifications include comprehensive experience in the analysis and resolution of administered and organizational problems, staffing studies and changes, personnel training and supervisor retraining, and establishing short- and long-term goals.

Skilled communications specialist with the ability to recognize a variety of perspectives and visualize the scope and impact of a program, both independently and in relation to other providing services.

(See resume on page 148.)

SKILLS & EQUIPMENT

There are three types of skills as far as the resume is concerned: those absolutely necessary to do the job, those that might help but that you can get by without, and those that are nice but have nothing to do with the job's requirements.

A fairly recent development in resume writing is to mention computer skills, as there seems to be some value in any degree of experience in operating or programming. List the brand and model numbers of the equipment you have worked with. Include only skills in which you are accomplished and proficient.

EXAMPLES

Experienced in key-entry and DTC for
banking operations.
Recognition Equipment:
REI 5400 & 7400 Keyscans.
Image Processors:
Mohawk & Technikron & Banctec.

Systems Analysis:
IBM 360 & 370 & HP 3000
S/370 Facilities & O.S. System Control
CICS & IMS & LINR & IBM Utilities S-170

Cameras: 2¼ × 2¼ 4 × 5;
View; Milliken DBM Hi-Speed.

Quad Eight Mixing Board
Nagra II, IV, IV-S.
Orban Sybalance Controller
Sportmaster Cart Machine

Wood Carving & Masonry & Glass Etching
Arc & Acetylene Welding

LICENSES & CERTIFICATION

In many professions, such as real estate, insurance, education, or stockbroking, a license is a requirement for certain positions. Present your credentials even if it would be assumed you would posseses the necessary certification. List only current and related licenses, and be prepared to show proof of such claims.

EXAMPLES

Kansas Real Estate Licenses: Broker (1992) & Salesman (1990).

Presently hold 5th issue of U.S. Coast Guard Master's License.

Certified School Teacher (K–6), State of Iowa, 1992.
Registered Social Worker (#A1558); expires in 1995.

Associate & Fellow Certificates, New York Institute of Credit.

Student Pilot (1980) & Private Pilot (1985)
Instrument Pilot (1986) & Commercial Pilot (1987)
Flight Instructor (1988) & Commercial Multiengine (1990)
Biennial Checkride (1991) & 2nd Class Medical (1992)

Certified Health Physicist (1987) & Certified Paramedic
Instructor (1992). Examiner's License (Illinois, 1988; Michigan, 1992; Ohio, currently pending).

AFFILIATIONS & MEMBERSHIPS

This type of information is rarely important to interviewers. They can't tell from the resume if your association with professional or community groups is by necessity or for altruistic purposes. If you want to include such data, trim the list of activities to those which are most current.

Here's an example of a typical problem: overkill.

BEFORE

Community Services:

1987—Kennewick Soccer League, Fullback Coach for Shooting Stars
1976–1978—Downingtown Jaycees, Active & Assoc. Member, Chairman & Treasurer
1976—American Cancer Society, Industrial & Private Business Chairman
1977—Cystic Fibrosis Research Foundation, Public Chairman of Brandywine Bowl

1977—Friends of Downingtown Public Library, Public Relations Chairman

1981–1982—Chairman of Oak Cliff (Dallas) Soccer Carnival

1981–1982—Coach of under 14 girls soccer team—Oak Cliff Rockets

1983–1984—Club Commissioner and Coach of under 12 girls soccer (Team Div. Champion—St. Ann's Angels)

1986—Fullback Coach of under 16 girls soccer team (Div. Champions, N. Dallas Yellow Jackets)

1981–1986—Volunteer work with small businessmen in Mexican-American community

1981–1986—Established business procedures with Financial Records, etc.

AFTER

Community Activities

Volunteer work in the Mexican-American community. Coach for soccer teams; Soccer Club Commissioner. Public Relations

Committee Chairman, Friends of the Library. Member: Jaycees; Chamber of Commerce, American Heart Assn.

OTHER EXAMPLES

President of Memphis Home Builders Association during 1992 when recognized as "Fastest Growing Home Builders Association in the United States" and "Best HBA in the South."

Qualified member of Million Dollar Round Table (MDRT) 1992. Received five NSAAs, two HIQAs, and six NQAs. Member of American Insurance College Council.

Course Instructor—American Executives International "Negotiating Skills"—"How to Listen"—"Managing Stress"—"Finance and Accounting for Non-financial Administrators"

International Association of Hospitality Accountants Chairman, 22d Annual Convention President (1992) and Treasurer (1991)

LANGUAGES & TRAVEL

Proficiency in foreign languages may be the deciding factor in some jobs, such as international sales, import/export coordination, social work, or fund raising. Always describe your proficiency as fluent, working knowledge, or familiar with (meaning you could probably improve with some training).

Foreign travel other than holiday vacations adds to your worldview and makes the resume more interesting. Also, any experience as a resident of other countries highlights your expanded cultural awareness and the ability to cope with change and challenges.

EXAMPLES

Fluent Spanish (native of Cuba) and English (U.S. resident since 1962). Conversational French; some Arabic.

Accustomed to carrying on daily business transactions in Greek and Italian by overseas telephone.

Peace Corps worker in Central America and Africa. Excellent Spanish; working knowledge of Senegalese.

Traveled throughout Europe on bicycles with husband and two preschool children for five months in 1991–1992. Working knowledge of French and German.

BIODATA

Confused about personal data (now biodata)? It's not surprising. Everybody is. In the 1950s it was common to see resumes with not only photographs but personal items such as "own car and home" and "no dept encumbrances." The world of workers has changed radically since then and there's confusion in the wake. No one seems to know what to do: Attach a photograph? Mention age or sex? Show marital status? Say anything about religious or political activities? Note hobbies and interests?

PHOTOGRAPHS

Let's start with the easy one: NO PHOTOGRAPH. Unless you are a model, actor/actress, on-camera personality, or similar performer, the photograph serves no useful purpose. I have seen sales managers and mechanical engineers with photographs on their resumes, but I have never understood why. It always looked ridiculous no matter the integrity of the intent.

AGE & SEX

First names usually make it clear if you're male or female, but not always: Kim, Day, or J.L. can be either. If the name is a problem, identify yourself as Mr., Ms., or whatever you prefer. (It can be embarrassing when someone calls or writes and isn't quite sure!)

If you feel your age is preventing you from getting interviews, leave it off the resume along with the date of college graduation, military service, or jobs of more than 15 years ago. Construct your presentation on accessible skills and practical know-how. Consider your age as a minor aspect of your personal inventory.

MARITAL STATUS

Marital status generally has little bearing on qualifications for most jobs, so mention it only if you want to. However, for some jobs it may be relevant, such as a road sales rep who has to travel 75 percent. Saying you are "single" could help to obtain an interview, but on the other hand, saying you are a "mother of three children" may allow the employer to screen you out and save you the trouble of pursuing a job you could not accept anyway.

I cannot imagine anyone putting "divorced" or "separated" (or "living with someone" or "in between") on a resume. When in doubt, say nothing.

RELIGIOUS & POLITICAL ACTIVITIES

Ninety-nine percent of the time it's prudent to say nothing about this kind of personal involvement, even if it does show your interest in the community. One simply cannot be sure what a reader's reaction might be, so play it safe until the interview.

HOBBIES & INTERESTS

Unless your hobbies are so exotic and interesting that they really add some spice to the resume, don't bother taking up good space with such data. Stick to the meat of work and education.

REFERENCES & SALARY HISTORY

References usually don't belong on a resume. They should be typed on a separate sheet and provided at an interview after you have been asked for them. Never use a person's name without their explicit approval, and remember that a good reference may wear down with time. No one has any reason to check your references until there is mutual interest established and you are close to being hired, so just put "references upon request" at the bottom of the resume. (And even this may be deleted if you need the space for something more important.)

When providing references a list of three to five is enough, preferably professionals outside your trade and people who have known you a year or more. (A banker, lawyer, C.P.A., doctor, community leader, or clergyman are safe bets.) Be sure to give the correct mailing address and current telephone number.

A former or present employer may be included in

the list if the individual is a personal acquaintance; otherwise, the list should represent people who know you outside the workplace. Prospective employers reserve the right to check into your employment background as a routine matter.

Because a lot of classified advertisements ask for a salary history (or requirements) to accompany the resume, many applicants are confused about how to deal with this somewhat delicate situation. It's a double bind. On one hand, you do not want to price yourself out of a good job (at least not on the first shot), nor do you want to price yourself too low and get less than what the company is prepared to pay.

The fact is, it just doesn't make much sense to tell them exactly what you expect to be paid before you find out more about the job. Still, you must tell them something.

The standard technique most of my clients employ is to state the requirements or history in the rough fashion of "$30–40,000 range" or "mid-$50,000s" or "$35K Base + Commissions." This can start the negotiations while allowing for bargaining space.

If you feel driven to provide a complete salary history (after the initial interview, for example), follow the outline below:

1991–PRESENT
Regional Sales Manager $40K + Bonus
1990–1991
Regional Sales Rep $34K + Comm.
1987–1990
Store Manager (REVCO) $28K–$32K

1985–1987
Line Supervisor (BELL) $23K Finish
$19K Start

Say nothing about salary if you don't have to, or deal with it tactfully in a good cover letter. If you can, wait until you're asked.

PART TWO

SUMMARIES

PRESENTING YOUR CASE

We've all seen Perry Mason wrap up a tough case with a masterful summary of who did what, where, when, and how. He appeals to the sensitivity of the judge and jury; his final summing up pleads for understanding and attempts to make a complex story clear. The summary on a resume tries to do the same thing: present the facts in the most persuasive manner. However, in the courtroom the summary comes last, after the evidence is introduced. On the resume it comes first, serving as both the evidence and the objective.

A summary can tell a lot—and at the right place—where the first impression is made. Like an audition, doing it right the first time may make all the difference.

Ideally, your professional qualifications and personal attributes should suggest why you want a specific job and convince the objective reader you deserve it.

Personal attributes are particular traits you possess

that contribute significantly to your success in certain types of endeavors. For instance, a typical phrase used to describe a manufacturing plant manager is "shirt-sleeve," which sounds odd if you don't recognize (as most personnel managers would) the underlying connotation: a regular Joe who doesn't mind getting his hands dirty to get the job done properly and on schedule. Not the three-piece-suit—executive type, no prima donna, but a "can do" guy.

There are other personality traits that can be brought into the qualifications profile: "detail-oriented" (accountants, travel agents, draftsmen); "self-starter" (a road salesman doing his daily grind); "quick learner" (office assistant, word processor).

The summary is also an excellent vehicle for dealing with some typical problems: a series of unrelated jobs, periods of unemployment between jobs, or education without a formal degree.

Here's an analysis of one of my client's experience and qualifications. He just turned 40 and he has a vast knowledge of commercial construction. He's been in the business since he was a teenager, and now he has considerable "hands-on" experience. His work history encompasses numerous projects for many companies, starting as a framing carpenter to his current job as project manager for the construction of luxury homes.

In order to summarize his overall qualifications effectively, we need only to list his functional title and the type of projects he's managed. No details. As can be seen, it takes only two lines to state his goals and four lines to recap his experience.

Director of Operations
Residential & Commercial Construction

Homes up to $4,000,000 & Apartment Complexes

Conventional & Spec & Multi-Family

Medical Clinics & Strip Centers

Duplexes & Townhouses

There is no need to indicate the number of years experience he offers because it is irrelevant. Expertise is not measured in years alone. We have covered a broad range in the first introduction; now we tie it down.

Major Qualifications
Project Management

Financial Control & Multi-Project Monitoring

P&L Administration

Computerized Cost Analysis & Contract Management

Field Supervision & Problem Solving

These primary functional areas contain a lengthy list of particular responsibilities he has held. In an interview he can focus on and embellish certain areas a prospective employer may be interested in.

We continue to pound away, making our case and showing how his "can do" approach gets the job accomplished the way it is supposed to be. His "style" (in essence, the ability to overcome incessant problems) is part of the package.

Management Style

Long hours, hard work, lots of pressure, endless flow of changing details on 6–10 full-fledged projects for clients who can afford the best and want results, not excuses.

Accustomed to working vis-à-vis with people at the top (president of a $500,000,000 company) to salaried labor. Unique combination of hands-on construction trades experience and operations management skills.

His salary requirements are hinted at. He wants to screen out prospective employers who aren't willing to pay top dollar for top performance. He has no time for anything less than serious interest.

Requirements

Salary and incentive plan reflecting the real value of my expertise, energy, and reliability in a demanding role.

The following examples demonstrate the variety of narrative formats for summaries, and the different data headings that can be used. Here's a quick list of the usual ones:

Experience Overview

Summary of Qualifications

Professional Summary

Background Synopsis

Profile

Employment Highlights

Career Path

Track Record

Major Achievements

Personal Profile

EXAMPLES OF SUMMARIES

Experience Overview
Configuration Engineer

Articulate communicator with record of excellence in the field of engineering. Team leader for many projects:
Configuration Engineering
Systems Technical Analysis
Procurement & Negotiations

MAJOR INTERESTS Electrical Power. Shipping or Shipbuilding. Research (Marine/ Ecology). Export/Import.

STRENGTHS Management/administration of technical and financial concerns employing inventive problem solving.

SUMMARY OF QUALIFICATIONS
Marine Operations & Traffic Control
*Technical Consultant—Operations
[Equipment & Personnel]
Marine Harbor Pilotage & Training
Fire & Safety Procedures*

PROFESSIONAL SUMMARY
Fifteen years of in-depth analysis and planning in corporate finance and business development. Demonstrated skills in product planning and line cost control, cash management, forecasting, financial reporting, budgeting, debt financing, tax research, and P&L analysis.

1990–PRESENT—Budget Director [STATE AGENCY]
1989–1990—Finance Director, FOMCO INTERNATIONAL
1986–1989—Financial Analyst, EXXON
1984–1986—Product Manager, I.M.T.
1977–1984—MBA/BBA with Honors, HARVARD

Background Synopsis
Construction Superintendent

Construction Superintendent and Project Manager with a wide range of project experience from start-up through completion, including: apartments, offices, warehouses, shopping malls, recreation centers.

Background encompasses negotiations with and evaluation of subcontractors, payment authorization, purchasing, hiring/firing, security, and compliance with OSHA rules.

PROFILE
Professional administrator and successful business executive with extensive contacts in commerce and industry, Christian communities and the clergy.
Well-versed in the art of public relations and in formulating strategies to achieve financial goals and corporate objectives.

Employment Highlights
United States Air Force

Commissioned Officer in command of a HAWK Missile Battery with complete responsibility for 130 men, $15,000,000 in equipment, and a continuous 24-hour operational commitment.

Capabilities: site selection and operational activation; contractual review and change-orders; purchasing and logistics; transportation; equipment maintenance; personnel.

Career Path

1990–PRESENT—Marketing Specialist (Tax Packages)
1988–1990—Account Executive, DEAN WITTER
1987–1988—Mother
1985–1987—Account Executive Trainee
1981–1985—Corporate Sales Manager
1979–1981—Regional Sales Representative

TRACK RECORD
Positions with Pizza Hut over the past five years include: Director of Administration (2½ years), Director of Franchise Training (1½ years), and Regional Operations Specialist (1 year).
A people-oriented leader, results-type planner; articulate and analytical; hands-on manager able to control details. Exceptional organizational and problem-solving abilities; effective written and verbal communicator.

Major Achievements
Staff Specialist—Media Distribution
Designed and implemented computer-assisted human resource management systems for 6,000 employees (including Affirmative Action accounting).

Set up major data network components and initiated "soft line" concepts using the latest telecommunications theories and "hard line" practices.

Enacted new and innovative problem solving methodologies resulting in 29% renewal rate for major carriers.

Detail Sales—Pharmaceuticals
Available Immediately. Will Travel & Relocate.

STORE MANAGER ready for a "take-charge" position requiring a self-starter and experienced decision maker.
Experience: Planning, Budgeting, Bid Analysis, Contracting, Design, and Remodeling.

Plant Manager
Plastics & Injection Molding
Offering fourteen years of plant supervisory experience: set-up of original pilot plants and high-speed production facilities, purchasing of raw materials and manufacturing equipment, design of special machinery, and quality control.

Experienced in compliance requirements of USDA, FDA, ICC.

Corporate Development/Planning [Name & Address]
Financial Management/Treasury _____
Commercial Banking _____

Mother of three happy and healthy children who has been able to accumulate business skills while rearing a family.

Personal attributes: a high sense of regard for the feelings and needs of others and an enthusiasm for learning and doing the best job possible.

OBJECTIVE Qualified for a top-level management position with a growth-oriented, small-to-medium size manufacturer, preferably in furniture, woodworking, or related field.

SUMMARY Five years as Technical Director of major furniture manufacturing operations. Eight years as CEO of a company I developed into a major contract-furniture manufacturing plant.

PROFILE Ability to recognize and resolve conflicts in all functional areas; able to search out new profit approaches and inspire organizational cooperation. Have traveled extensively; work easily with all levels of management.

Printing Industry Experience

Twenty-five years in the Printing Industry specializing in cost studies (particularly production center operating costs) and in-depth profit/loss analyses.

Hands-on experience in virtually every phase and facet of print production of all types: publications, business forms, advertising agency work, and the diverse realm of general printing.

Experienced in offset sheet fed, web offset, and letterpress, as well as 6-color runs.

Flight Attendant with major airline for two
decades and twelve years of supervisory responsibilities for a crew of ten on-board personnel.

In addition to the full spectrum of public relations
skills required in this position, an expertise in cop-
ing quickly and tactfully with diverse problems
was essential, as could be expected when dealing
daily with people of all ages from across the world.

Programmer & Production Support Analyst
Operations Experience

   IBM 3084 MVS/XA
   IBM 3420 (Tape Drives)
   IBM 3081 MVS/XA
   IBM 3800 (Laser Printer)
   IBM 3380 (Disk Drives)
   IBM 3203 (Impact Printers)

Property Manager
Extensive experience in all aspects of residential
and commercial property management, including:
Budgeting & Forecasting, Leasing & Contract
Negotiations, Purchasing & Billing, Personnel
Supervision, Expense Reports, Profit Analysis,
Maintenance Programs.

Installation & Test Specialist
Offering more than twenty years of technical expertise and on-site management experience in the
following areas:

*1A Key—1A2 Key—756A—755—757
770—701—800—801—805—812
Horizon 16 & 32—Dimension 100—400
Concentrator/Identifier—Autotas—ECD
Step-by-Step Central Office—E.S.S.
Central Office—101 E.S.S.
PBX—Carrier Types including K, C, O, N, O/N,
N1 & T-2 wire/4 wire & toll switching circuits.*

Assistant Treasurer

Extensive knowledge of treasury operations and negotiating responsibilities, financial modeling and planning, present value analysis, mergers and acquisitions. M.B.A. in Finance and Quantitative Analysis; B.B.A. in Economics.

Restaurant Manager

Restaurant Manager with more than eight years of experience in all aspects of restaurant management including:

catering preparation/management

food & beverage purchasing

inventory & stock control

personnel hiring & training

menu planning & pricing

bar operations management

bookkeeping & banking

quality control & housekeeping

TRAVEL AGENT: SABRE, Reservations, Ticketing/Tariffs, CLIA Certification, World Geography, International/Domestic Routing, Professional Development, Application of OAGs.

Marketing/Public Relations

Offering more than four years of marketing and public relations experience, with professional skills in:

Sales Presentations

Feasibility Studies

Customer Relations

Training & Promotions

Management

Engineer

Reconnaissance & Electro-Optical/Infrared

Technical Manuals/Orders & Maintenance Procedures

Training & Methods

Top Secret Clearance

Position Desired
Option, Listed or OTC Trader.
Experience

6 Years—Option Trader

4 Years—OTC Trader

8 Years—Registered Representative

Member of New York S.T.A. since 1982

OBJECTIVE:
A responsible position in a law firm as a legal secretary or researcher.

PERSONAL ATTRIBUTES:
Able to deal with clients and staff in a professional and friendly manner despite conditions of deadlines and pressure. Possess practical sense of priorities and the action needed to finish a task.

Executive Housekeeper
Offering seven years of housekeeping management experience, including grand openings, budget forecasting, hiring and training, inventory, purchasing, and payroll.

Hotels

Loew's Anatole & Plaza of the Americas

Hyatt Regency & The Fairmount

Experience Highlights

ADMINISTRATION & MANAGEMENT

Experienced in supervising the daily operations of administrative offices as well as planning/scheduling activities.

PERSONNEL

Experienced manager of people and accomplished in setting up training programs. Adept interviewer and personnel evaluator with the ability to maintain productive employee relations.

TEACHING

Classroom instructor with a strong background in working community organizations and developing new educational programs.

Computer Engineering Specialist

Broad experience and expertise in systems troubleshooting and maintenance, technical support, and the installation of Engineering Work Orders. Fully accustomed to working independently with decision-making responsibilities.

Management Consultant

Nursing home management consultant with experience in staff training/upgrading and program planning. Familiar with the State of Missouri and HEW standards and procedures and State Welfare recertification assessments.

PART THREE

EXAMPLES OF RESUMES

COMMENTS

The following 40 resumes show the great variety of formats available. They range from standard and traditional designs to newer formats. There are 14 resumes that have accompanying letters in Part Five. They are all one-page formats, except for the resume on page 148.

RESUME PAGE	LETTER PAGE
109	201
110	202
111	199
112	200
113	204
115	212
116	206
118	203
119	205
121	207
138	208

139	209
144	210
146	211

Resumes on pages 109–134 are those of people already at work in the business world, generally with 3 to 15 years of experience. Resumes on pages 135–142 are those of students. Resumes on pages 143–149 are for people in military service.

The resume on page 124 is an example of a *presentation format*. It has been custom designed for one particular company (and their name is on the resume so they'll know it was made just for them). This is a very effective technique for showing a prospective employer that you are putting out your best efforts.

Susan Jane Hemingway
4 Park Hill Drive #235
Des Moines, Iowa 50312
(515) 246-3844

Primary Objective
SALES REPRESENTATIVE

Seeking an opportunity to start a new career in sales, and in particular, a chance to demonstrate a high level of motivation to succeed. Willing to travel (no restrictions).

Personal attributes include the ability to work well with people from all walks of life, and the capacity to function independently with own decision-making responsibilities.

College Education
Bachelor of Business Administration in Marketing, 1990.
Bachelor of Science in Health Education, 1986.
UNIVERSITY OF IOWA

Work Experience
[Business]

TRANSCON LINES, Iowa City (1989–Present) & Time-D.C., Inc., Webster City (1981–1986). Coordinator and supervisor of freight shipping operations, including: organizing work flow and assigning personnel; reports (manifests and logs); preparation of work for oncoming shift; problem solving; line-haul scheduling.

[Education]

IOWA CITY INDEPENDENT SCHOOL DISTRICT (1986–1989). Teacher at Wilson Middle School and JFK Junior High School: curriculum planning and development; class instruction; assistant coach (three sports); assisting counselors and students in program planning and career guidance; records maintenance; organizing field trips to local businesses.

Active in Honors and Work-Study program guideline development. Responsible for maintaining constant contact with participating companies and evaluating progress of students.

Biodata
Born 23 January 1955. Single. Excellent health.

References Furnished Upon Request

Kathy Ann Alsobrook
699 Gainsboro Avenue Detroit, Michigan 48220
HOME 313/443-2398 SERVICE 313/239-9874

CAREER OBJECTIVE

A role in the field of marketing, public relations, or business management where a background in business and psychology may be utilized.

Seeking an opportunity to gain additional experience in planning and implementing creative management strategies.

EDUCATIONAL EXPERIENCE

Graduate School of Management, University of Michigan.

Courses in Marketing Management and Financial Accounting.
September 1989–June 1990.

University of Michigan.

Bachelor of Arts with concentration in Psychology.
Graduated in 1987. Dean's List (GPA: 3.5).

OCCUPATIONAL EXPERIENCE

Department of Human Resources, Ann Arbor. 1991–Present

Caseworker specializing in incest intervention and treatment. Accountable for analyzing family dynamics and designing individual service plans. Responsible for planning and implementing therapy groups for adult offenders. Direct involvement in civil and criminal court proceedings requiring thorough research of legal issues and professional presentation of case material.

Volunteers in Probation, Ann Arbor. 1991

Worked with Program Director to develop and coordinate community-based program. Recruited, trained, and supervised seven volunteers who counseled and tutored juvenile offenders. Assisted in preparing department's annual grant application.

Washtenaw Co. Public Defender's Office, Ann Arbor. 1990

Interviewed clients and witnesses, coordinated evidence in preparation for trial, and investigated placement options for sentencing recommendations.

Bell, Harnes & Breeden, Cleveland, Ohio. Summer 1988

General office manager for prominent law firm: research and coordination of inter-office communications.

REFERENCES ON REQUEST

John Loughlin
4200 Hyannis Drive   Richmond, Virginia 23235   393-4502

COMPUTER ENGINEERING SPECIALIST

Broad experience and expertise in systems troubleshooting and maintenance, technical support, and the installation of Engineering Change Orders. Fully accustomed to working independently.

FIELD SERVICE EXPERIENCE
June 1990 to Present
CompuServices, Incorporated Home Office: Columbus, Ohio

Field Engineer

Field Engineer I (6/90–11/91) working out of the Columbus Office. Promoted to Field Engineer II and assigned to the Roanoke, Virginia Office (11/91–Present).

Function independently and report to Field Supervisor in the Washington, D.C. Office. Specific territorial responsibility for Virginia, West Virginia, and Maryland. Provide technical support and troubleshooting for Fortune 1000 companies using CompuServices networking.

May 1986 to June 1990
Infodetics Corporation
Home Office: Huntsville, Alabama

Electronics Field Service Technician

Worked in Detroit (1986–1988) and then assigned to Huntsville (1988–1990). Functioned independently with overall responsibility for providing technical support and electronics troubleshooting.

TECHNICAL TRAINING

Successfully completed formal training programs at CompuServices and Infodetics. Completed advanced courses in Electronics at Thomas Nelson Community College (Hampton, Virginia) and Ohio Institute of Technology at Columbus.

Coulter Electronics Models School (1983). Becton Dickinson ARIAII Automated RIA School (1984). "Introduction to TI-PASCAL" and "990/DS10 ASSEMBLY" at Sperry Vickers.

References: Available Upon Request

Minerva ("Min") Vasquez
12   Mescal   Court   Tucson,   Arizona   85718   (602)   385-9932

PROPERTY MANAGER

Extensive experience in all facets of residential/commercial property management: Budgeting & Forecasting, Leasing & Contract Negotiations, Purchasing & Billing, Personnel Hiring & Supervision, Expense Reports & Profit Analysis.

EMPLOYMENT HISTORY

Tri-State Properties, Inc., Phoenix, 1990–Present.

Property Manager for 230 commercial and residential properties, including 14 apartment complexes throughout the Phoenix metropolitan area.

Barclay Management Co., Phoenix, 1987–1990.

Property Manager for a total of 712 units: Desert Flower Apartments, Four Corners Complex, Statler Hills, Clover Glen.

Traveled to Memphis and Nashville on special assignments to set up renovation programs for other Barclay properties.

Majestic Realty Co., Austin, Texas, 1985–1987.

Resident Property Manager for a total of 310 units at Pleasant Village Apartments and Cedar Grove Apartments. Supervised construction of four new swimming pools and recreation areas.

Northern Telecom, Houston, Texas, 1981–1984.

Project Coordinator for the construction of computer printing systems throughout the United States.

Held "Top Secret" clearance. Coordinated and set up sites and assisted in organizing union and contractual agreements for numerous projects ($3,750,000 each).

Xerox Corporation, Chicago & Denver, 1979–1981.
Telex Corporation, Chicago, 1979.

Field Service Engineer, Computers.

EDUCATION & TRAINING

Control Data Institute (Chicago): "Computer Technology," 1977.
Business Methods Institute (Chicago): "Engineering Applications."
Courses in "Business Law/Administration" at various schools.

Robert B. Hamilton
217 Sequoia Road NW
Albuquerque, New Mexico 87120
(505) 459-1988
Business: 229-1988

OBJECTIVE

Transportation Management

Seeking a position drawing upon ten years' experience in the transportation
and trucking industry. Strong track record of increasing responsibilities and
effective management.

WORK EXPERIENCE

1991 to Present
Alcron Systems, Inc., Albuquerque.
Corporate Services Division

WAREHOUSE MANAGER. Responsible for management of receiving,
shipping, delivery, storage, and general material handling. Supervise 35–50
full- and part-time personnel (including supervisors and crew leaders); hire/
train employees; quality control; equipment maintenance; problem solving.

Successfully reorganized both shipping and receiving departments with
complete tracking system and much improved receiving procedures for
inventory control.

Implemented a new safety and licensing program for all forklift operators reducing accidents by 60%.

1987 to 1991
American North Atlantic, Boston.

SPECIAL PROJECTS DIRECTOR. Responsible for developing the Office
Moving Division: coordinated all office moves and worked with sales staff to
estimate time, cost, equipment, and personnel needs. Trained supervisors
and other employees; maintained fleet of trucks and related moving equipment.

1985 to 1987
Central Moving & Storage, Boston.

SUPERVISOR. Responsible for personnel supervision, training, and daily
operations, including paperwork and customer service.

1982 to 1985
Driver for Vernon Schmidt Moving Services, Philadelphia.
Driver for Buckley Storage Co., Philadelphia.

Marilyn Scott-Brenner
Post Office Box 2399
310 Sewanee Boulevard
Cleveland, Ohio 44146
(216) 545-3299

PROFESSIONAL OBJECTIVE

To utilize my broad base of business and managerial background in the areas of finance and home-related sales.

Available immediately. Willing to relocate (no restrictions).

COLLEGE EDUCATION

Bachelor of Business Administration in Accounting, 1987.

Minors in Real Estate and Finance, GPA: 3.7
CASE WESTERN UNIVERSITY
-Phi Eta Sigma & Blue Key National Honorary Society
-Hogg-McAtee Academic Scholarship

EMPLOYMENT HISTORY

CUSTOM BILT POOLS (Cleveland), February 1992–Present.

Sales Representative

Responsible for new pool design and sales in the Cleveland metropolitan area.
(Salary plus commission.)

CLEVELAND COURIER SERVICES, 1983–1992.
[Full-time summers, part-time during school.]

Accounting Branch Supervisor (1991–1992)

Supervised general accounting functions, including:

C.O.D. Cash Collections ($175,000+ daily)
Accounts & Claims Payable
Payroll (180 employees)
Fuel & Oil Accounting
General Ledger
Journals & Reconciliations
Monthly Accounting Statements
Outside Audit Preparations

Data Processing Supervisor (1989–1991)

HUB Supervisor/Unloader (1982–1989)

REFERENCES

Excellent references provided upon request.

Johnny K. Madison
41 Confederate Lane
Atlanta, Georgia 30341
(404) 522-1990

PROFESSIONAL EXPERIENCE

2/92–Present **Senior Account Executive**
Corporate Showrooms/Atlanta
Sales of shared tenant services to wholesale dealers in the
Atlanta Showplace. Top salesman in second month of
employment.

7/91–2/92 **Account Services Specialist**
Sharecome Incorporated/Atlanta
Sales of long distance services for shared tenant services
company. Helped develop an auto-dialer program and
installed dialers. Exceeded sales quotas and sold the
company's top two accounts.

3/89–5/91 **Marketing Representative**   MCI/Lexington, Kentucky
Opened up new market and sold long distance services.
Met or exceeded established sales quotas consistently.

1988–1989 **Paralegal/Law Clerk**   Houston & Willows/Atlanta
Part-time paralegal while studying at college. Researched
and drafted briefs on cases; courthouse liaison work.

1986–1987 **Account Executive**   KKKW-FM Radio/Atlanta
Sold advertising time to direct and agency accounts. Wrote
creative copy and presented advertising plans. Compiled
media statistical reports on local audience.

1985–1986 **Account Executive**
KXIY-TV (ABC)/Lexington, Kentucky
Sold advertising to local and regional accounts. Developed
schedules, wrote copy, assisted in production. Attended
national ABC convention as KXIY representative.

1984–1985 **Assistant to Personnel Manager**
Tribeca Manufacturing/Atlanta
Worked summers in family-owned business.

Formal B.A. in Radio/TV Communications, 1985.
Education Georgia Southwestern College

Annie Boyd
121 Mountain Valley Road
Portland, Oregon 97229
(503) 340-4876

JOB OBJECTIVE

Managerial position commensurate with seven years of experience in sales and operations management, customer service, and personnel supervision.

BUSINESS BACKGROUND
1990 to Present

HERBS-FOR-LIVING INTERNATIONAL
Portland Regional Office

SALES ORDERS SUPERVISOR

Responsible for supervision of operations in the Portland Distribution Center which is linked to eighteen U.S. distribution centers and five in foreign countries.

Complete charge of personnel (73) in five departments: Telephone Sales; Credit Card; Wire Transfer; Customer Service; Mail Order. Heavy emphasis on problem solving and detail tracking and coordination.

1986 to 1990

SEARS ROEBUCK & COMPANY

Portland Store

SERVICE CENTER SUPERVISOR Responsible for 22 employees in three departments, as well as customer relations, problem solving, and work scheduling.

CONTRACT SALES: Sold appliances commercially to companies in the Portland area.

Seattle Store

MAINTENANCE AGREEMENT SALES: Sold service contracts (new and unsold categories).

Education

Completed 45 hours of Liberal Arts and Business Management courses at Cedar Valley College in Lancaster, Texas, 1981–1984.

References Upon Request

Confidential Resume

LOURDES TORRES

24 Frontenac South   Seattle, Washington 98108   (206) 357-3975

PROFESSIONAL GOAL

To continue my career in Property Tax Research.

SYNOPSIS OF QUALIFICATIONS

Adept communicator as a result of business experience and college training; detail oriented and strong on accuracy and problem solving. Excellent customer service skills; able to represent a company in a positive professional manner.

BUSINESS EXPERIENCE

October 1991 to Present

Grayson Realty Tax Services—Seattle

Tax Researcher & Team Leader

Report directly to the Senior Tax Researcher. Team Leader in charge of Bill Processing Team (7–14 people) during tax season. Primary responsibilities:

> problem solving and related public relations through daily contact with customers and tax agencies
> researching information concerning contracts and loans using a CRT (IBM system)
> obtaining legal descriptions of properties and name(s) of owner(s)
> troubleshooter and liaison between mortgage companies and taxing authorities (Washington & Oregon)

EDUCATION & OTHER EXPERIENCE

Bachelor of Arts in Social Work—1990
UNIVERSITY OF WASHINGTON

Volunteer Work: Big Sister Program; Special Olympics; Tri-County Human Services Coalition; Community Action Program/Urban Development; Wishard Hospital.

Work experience: teacher's assistant; library assistant; salesperson. Earned 100% of college expenses.

REFERENCES AVAILABLE

Letitia Honowantine
77 Ridgeway Lane   Apartment #211   Denver, Colorado   (303) 438-9580

POSITION DESIRED
Junior Programmer or Production Support Analyst

OPERATIONS EXPERIENCE

IBM 3084 MVS/XA	IBM 3380 (Disk Drive)	IBM 3800 (Laser Printer)
IBM 3081 MVS/XA	IBM 3420 (Tape Drive)	IBM 3203 (Impact Printer)

SPECIAL TRAINING
Advanced Systems Inc. & Deltak Inc.: Completed several courses in JCL and COBOL, Video and System Operator Training.

COLLEGE EDUCATION
University of Hawaii at Honolulu, B.S., Data Processing, 1986.

EMPLOYMENT
1988 to Present

Snowy Snacks Incorporated/Denver

3/92–Present: Promoted to SENIOR OPERATOR with responsibility for being familiar with Computer Room Shutdown, Emergency Backup Battery System, and Halon Sprinkler System. Trained in Production Support using JCL as a Backup Analyst. Assist supervisor in scheduling operators: Acting Supervisor when needed.

Major Responsibilities: Alter initiator structure to maintain throughput; perform unscheduled initial program load and stand-alone dump procedures; analyze first-stage operational problems and take appropriate action; notify responsible vendors when required.

Assist in training operators on tape drives, printers, procedures; log abnormal endings of jobs; log downtime/hardware trouble.

1989–3/92: Promoted to COMPUTER OPERATOR on IBM 370 mainframe and peripherals. Trained new operators; ran two master consoles (test and production system with IMS); insured good job mix in system.

Monitored the UCC7 scheduling package; notified Production Support of any late jobs and scheduling discrepancies. Brought up systems after failures and insured that all appropriate software packages were active, including: UCC7, UCC71-COM, IMSPROD, NCCF, NETBLK, NETRED, OMEGAMON, CICS, TDVSMSX, TSO, JHS, IMSTEST, JES2, AFM.

Additional Details Provided in Interview

Confidential
MICHAEL BENEDICT COTTONE
164-E Volvo Circuit Road   Bethesda, Maryland 20014   (301) 444-1963

Objective
A position in HYDRAULICS ELECTRONICS drawing upon extensive experience in the areas of installation, inspection, and field service.

Work Experience

1990–Present   City of Bethesda   **Instrument Technician**
Employed as a Construction Inspector (2/90–9/90) and became an Apprentice Instrument Technician; following six months of apprenticeship was promoted to present position.
Responsibilities: troubleshooting and repair of water pressure transmitters, flow transmitters, and water tank level transmitters and receivers. Use VOM multimeters, mercury and tube manometers to test signals that are transmitted through phone lines to a central computer.

1985–1990   Parkan-Denton Company   **Field Service Representative**
Responsible for installing PD drills to exact specifications and training employees in the operation and maintenance of new drills and upkeep and major overhauls of old models. Assisted in locating spare parts and advised engineers on technical problems.
Traveled to Chile, Spain, Norway, Canada, Mexico, and across the U.S.A. to resolve difficult problems. In addition, helped rewrite/update PD service manuals for the following PD models:

PD 120:   track-mounted; bit loading to 125,000 lbs.; working weight of 300,000 lbs.; 22″ hole.

PD 100:   track-mounted; electric powered; bit loading to 125,000 lbs.; working weight of 250,000 lbs.; 17½″ hole up to 275 ft. deep.

PD 70:   track-mounted rig with bit loading to 70,000 lbs.; electric/diesel powered.

PD 60:   tire-mounted rig with bit loading to 60,000 lbs. and 120,000 lbs. working weight; diesel/electric powered.

Positions: F.S. Rep (1988–1990). Hydraulic Assembler (1987–1988) training apprentices testing drills. Apprentice (1986–1987) on large blast hole drills. Material handler/fork lift operator (1985–1986). Power saw operator.

References Upon Request

Confidential	Do Not Contact Present Employer

Roscoe E. Thompson   **(201) 497-6344**

PROFESSIONAL EXPERIENCE

Hotel Management Systems (New York City)
Special Projects, Corporate Office
Jan. 1992–Present

Acting controller (3/92–present) of a 550-room hotel with two restaurants and three beverage outlets. Helped with purchase of the hotel and developed an accounting staff of 14 people; set up accounting systems and reporting procedures.

Closing consultant (1/92–3/92) helping close former property that was sold.

Controller
Ramada Inn/Galveston, Texas
June 1991–Nov. 1991

Supervised the accounting function for a 360-room group/transient hotel with two restaurants and two beverage outlets. In charge of all monthly, quarterly, and yearly reporting.

Controller
Dupont Plaza Hotel/Kansas City, Missouri
Oct. 1990–May 1991

Responsible for all accounting functions in a 244-room hotel. Supervised a staff of 9 and helped maintain records for four other companies.

Controller
Boston Hilton Inn, Boston, Massachusetts
March 1988–July 1990

Responsible for all accounting functions in a 350-room hotel. Set up new accounting systems for two companies and retrained staff of 26.

Controller
Hospitality Management Corporation,
Memphis, Tennessee
May 1986–Feb. 1988

Responsible for all accounting functions at five properties. Prepared all financial statements, trained an accounting staff, and held operational responsibilities.

Internal Auditor
Southern Hotels, Inc., Atlanta, Georgia
Apr. 1983–Apr. 1986

Internal auditor for ten properties. Instituted and reviewed controls and systems; trained new controller.

Education   Hotel Administration courses across the U.S.A.
References   Furnished after mutual interest is established.

Delilah Grace Williams
1600 High Line Drive
Birmingham, Alabama 35217
(205) 472-8892 [Messages]

POSITION SOUGHT
Secretary/Administrative Assistant

QUALIFICATIONS
Fully experienced in all facets of office procedures and policies. Mature and easygoing woman who has lots of experience in everything from fixing the coffee pot to calming down irate and threatening customers. Knows how to establish priorities.

READY TO WORK NOW

A Summary of Skills & Experience
Typing (120 WPM) & Speedwriting (90 WPM)
Daily Bookkeeping & Banking
G/L & P/L & A/R & A/P
Corporate Minutes & Contracts
Presentations Design & Printing & Binding
Recordkeeping & Filing & Correspondence
Word Processing & Data Research
Telex & CRT & 10-Key
Dun & Bradstreet & Salesmen's Reports

And Much More

PRIMARY EMPLOYERS SINCE 1982
Titles: Ranged from Secretary to Executive V.P. to Office Manager, Customer Service Expert, and IRS Liaison.

1990–1992: METRO FACTORS, INCORPORATED
1988–1990; BUENA VISTA DISTRIBUTION (Walt Disney Productions)
1987–1988: BARNES IMPORT CERAMICS
1987: AMERICAN AUTOMOBILE ASSOCIATION
1985–1987: REGIS AUTOMOBILE AGENCY
1982–1985: CHASE MANHATTAN
1981–1982: BOWERY SAVINGS & LOAN

RELATED TRAINING
Extensive list of courses at community colleges and in company-sponsored programs includes word processing, report writing, presentation design, audio/visual scripting, expense analysis.

Strictly Confidential

WILLIAM S. WILLOWBY
Post Office Box 443   Grant's Station Annex
Broken Arrow, Oklahoma 74012   (918) 234-8882

WORK EXPERIENCE

1991 to   **[A Major Petroleum Service]**
Present   **Staff Accountant**

Responsible for assisting client companies in all phases of Oil & Gas accounting, auditing of Federal Income Tax for integrity and availability of windfall profit tax refund potential due to over/under with provisions of the 90% Net Income Limitations.

Responsible for insuring clients' compliance with applicable Federal, State, and Local tax laws in addition to Internal Revenue Service codes regarding all phases of Oil & Gas accounting. Supervise Data Entry clerks in daily operations. Travel 95%.

Special Assignment: 10/91–3/92
Conversion Specialist

Assisted client companies with accounting computer conversion. Analyzed division orders, oil and gas mineral leases, royalty checks, mineral deeds, and 6248s. The documents were used to help company to correct mineral and land ownership records, tier classification, royalty payments, and legal land description for properties clients owned.

Also prepared masterfile, set up and keyed information into the system. Reorganized client Oil and Gas mineral files and performed research. Travel 85%.

1989–1991   **WESTERN OIL & GAS EXPLORATION—FT. WORTH**
                  Tax Accounting Analyst

Prepared and filed Federal, State, Local, and Out-of-State production taxes for all divisions and subdivisions for Oil and Gas purchases. Prepared voucher requisitions for payment of monthly Oil and Gas purchases and tax payments; miscellaneous research.

Prior   Bookkeeping for Consolidated Rail, summers 1986 &
Experience   1987.
                 Data collection coder, Indiana University, 1983–1985.

Education   B.S., Finance, Indiana University, 1987.

Equipment   HP Computer System; Keypunch; 10-Key; Data Point
                 1800.

Charles ("Corky") Cotrell

100 East Craig   Casper, Wyoming 33498   Phone (307) 259-3988

PROJECT ENGINEER/CONSTRUCTION SUPERINTENDENT

Offering extensive experience in MIS/MSS, budget control, personnel supervision, and equipment/facilities maintenance.

PROFESSIONAL EXPERIENCE

1981 TO 1992
WYOMING UTILITIES MINING COMPANIES

Maintenance Consultant to Mine Manager (1990–1992)

Responsibilities: special projects, budget control, contractors.

Senior Engineer (1986–1990)

Brighton & Tarpington Mining Operations

Organized, developed, and managed a maintenance department of 140 people (including 22 supervisors and 12 engineers/aides); total responsibility for a $26,000,000 annual budget.

The department maintained all mine-related equipment: draglines, loading shovels, hydraulic excavator, lignite processing facilities, coal haulers, Cat. 637 scrapers, front-end loaders, Cat. 149 motor-graders, dozers, maintenance shop/office facilities, and all related service vehicles and facilities.

Assistant Maintenance Engineer (1985–1986)

One of the original developers of the MIS/MSS systems within the company, which were used to identify 23,000 items and to control warehouse inventory and purchasing.

Responsibilities: all maintenance of stripping, loading, railroad, hauling, mine facilities, and support equipment. Direct supervision of engineers and technicians.

Staff Assistant to Mine Manager (1981–1985)

Budget and special projects coordinator: department manager of railroad operations; electric and diesel/electric locomotives (100-ton coal cars; 80-ton limestone cars; side-dump cars).

1976 TO 1981
SEATTLE POWER & LIGHT COMPANY

Associate & Commercial Engineer

Designed, organized, and coordinated planning/construction of power systems and equipment for numerous major commercial buildings.

Dennice Cameron
342 West 29th Street
Manchester, New Hampshire 03103
(603) 429-1147

Prepared For
HARMON-LAURANTINE, INCORPORATED
Manchester Retail Store

POSITION DESIRED
Salesperson

EMPLOYMENT HISTORY
June 1991 to Present
EMPLOYEES FEDERAL CREDIT UNION
Manchester Main Office

Teller & Receptionist

Began as a receptionist in a branch office and was promoted to current position of teller in 1/92.

Responsibilities: assisting credit union members in balancing their accounts and conducting transactions (deposits, withdrawals, payments), as well as typing, filing, bookkeeping, and responding to questions on the telephone.

May 1989 to May 1991
BORDEN POLICE DEPARTMENT
COCTANE COUNTY SHERIFF'S OFFICE

Secretary & Dispatcher

Duties: Callboard dispatcher; recordkeeping, filing, typing, phone.

PERSONAL PROFILE
Able to relate to diverse people, read and speak some French. Neat and attractive appearance; enthusiastic worker. Canoe instructor. Attended New Hampshire Outward Bound School (1988).

LETTERS OF RECOMMENDATION UPON REQUEST

Rose Marie Catacalos
224 Elliot Place
San Francisco, California 94108
(415) 553-1233

PRODUCTION PATTERN MAKER
More than fifteen years of pattern making, clothing design, production,
and quality control experience in the USA/England.

FORMAL EDUCATION
City & Guild Certificates—1980
THE COLLEGE OF FASHION & CLOTHING TECHNOLOGY
London, England

EMPLOYMENT CHRONOLOGY
1990 to Present
Production Pattern Maker
BOBBIE BROOKS CORPORATION & BRENNER/SALTY'S APPAREL
San Francisco & Los Angeles

1987 to 1990
Production Pattern Maker
L'TONARY & CALIFORNIA GIRL & TEN ONE
Los Angeles & San Diego

1985 to 1987
Production Manager
Pattern Maker & Clothing Technician
THE FIVE WEAVERS & CAREER WOMAN LTD.
Los Angeles

1976 to 1985
Designer & Pattern Maker
STANROSE OF LONDON

_____ Additional Details & Samples Upon Request _____

Lee Anne Sullenberger
333 Berkley Boulevard
New Orleans, Louisiana 70126
(504) 439-3499

SYNOPSIS OF PROFESSIONAL SKILLS

17-Keto-Steroids
17-Hydroxycorticosteroids
Paper & Thin Layer Chromatography
Column Chromatography, Silica Gel,
Florisil, LH-20, Sephadex
All Clinical Chemistry including Auto
Analyser, Astrup Blood Gases
Routine Hematology
Bone Marrow Preparation & Staining
of Smears
Serology
Electrophoresis
EKG

Radio Immuno Assays, Testosterone,
Dehydroepiandrosterone Sulfate,
17-OH Progesterone
Comparative Protein Binding
Assays—Testosterone,
Dehydroepiandrosterone Sulfate
Micro Methods for Pediatrics
Coulter Counter
Blood Bank & AIDS Search
Vanguard Strip Scanner
Liquid Scintillation Counter
Beckman DU Spectrophotometer
Coleman Spectrophotometer
Quality Control

EMPLOYMENT HISTORY

1991–Present	**Methodist General Hospital** [Dr. Myron Blackwell] *Lab Supervisor—Pediatric Endocrinology*
1989–1991	**Hollywood Medical Center** [Dr. Gretchen Graves; Dr. Jason Godwin] *Research Technologist*
1986–1989	**Kaiser Foundation** [Dr. L.H. White] *Lab Supervisor—Endocrinology*
1984–1986	**Beth Temple Children's Hospital** [Dr. Jon Van Kampenhein] *Biochemist—Clinical Chemistry*

EDUCATION & CERTIFICATION

1984	A.S.C.P. Registered Medical Technologist
1983	Bachelor of Science in Medical Technology UNIVERSITY OF CALIFORNIA AT LOS ANGELES

REFERENCES UPON REQUEST

Thomas Smith
[pseudonym]
P.O.B. 4199—Miami, Florida 33141   Home: 305/732-5399 (Evenings)

Objective   Upper management position in Marketing commensurate
with 20 years of successful consumer products experience.

Experience   Marketing administration/product management
Profile   background encompasses an extremely broad base of
domestic and international products, diverse selling
methods and distribution systems with a Fortune 500
corporation.

POSITION CHRONOLOGY

1981 to   [A LEADING U.S. SELLER OF FRUIT PRODUCTS]
Present   Miami • New York • San Francisco • Montreal

Director of Marketing Administration
TROPICAL PRODUCTS DIVISION/MIAMI   1991–Present

Group Products Manager
CANNED FRUITS DIVISION/MONTREAL   1989–1991

V.P., Director of Marketing
NEW PRODUCTS/CANADIAN MARKET   1988–1989

Director of Market Research
U.S. & CANADA PROGRAMS   1986–1988
—Health-Oriented Beverages   —Low Calorie Lines
—Repackaging/U.S. Regional   —Subsidiary Tie-in Programs

Executive Product Manager
U.S. MARKET/NEW YORK & MIAMI   1983–1986
—Bottled & Frozen Juices   —Bulk Sales

Product Manager
SOUTHEASTERN U.S. MARKET   1982–1983

Field Salesman & Product Analyst
EASTERN SEABOARD   1981–1982
ENGLAND: Special Research Project   CANADA: Market Studies

Education   M.B.A., B.B.A., University of Montreal.
Recent studies: "Dynamics of Motivational Management"
(Centex); "Point-of-Sale Breakovers" (Arlen).

CONFIDENTIAL REFERENCES FOLLOWING INTERVIEW

Arthur James Bernstein
2719 West Pecan Valley Drive   Charlotte, North Carolina 28210
HOME: 704-599-3299   OFFICE: 704-433-2760 Ext. 205

Objective
To direct contracted activities or to direct the allocation of resources and funds for continuing operations, special projects, or capital improvements.

Experience Summary
Progressive responsibility for contract management, operations analysis, and funds control. Familiar with the Federal Acquisition Regulations and industrial/commercial contracting practices.

Experienced in both service and technical product environments, including development and manufacture of complex aerospace test equipment. Administered contracts and controlled $50–$70 million budget for twelve facilities in seven states.

RELATED ACHIEVEMENTS

Program Planning
Designed a financial records system for comparison of budgeted and actual costs. Directed allocations and adjustments based on cost advantage analyses. Established one- and five-year advance action plans.

Contract Management
Established results-oriented engineering and manufacturing milestones leading to delivery of high technology equipment, with concurrent profit responsibility. Directed contract administration on 20–25 concurrent contracts, and negotiated awards and modifications.

Operations Analysis
Analyzed and identified operating problems for the conversion to cost equivalents and for comparison to alternative solution costs. Installed and evaluated cost efficient solutions.

Staff Development
Developed and conducted training programs for management staff. Prepared visual aids and written materials, and evaluated performance improvements.

Oral & Written Communications
Express ideas, directions, and analyses clearly and concisely. Comfortable in both theoretical and practical environments. Able to meet and deal on all levels.

Independence & Teamwork
Able to independently develop plans and systems consistent with staff goal. Responsive to suggestions and to criticism.

Security
Secret for ten years; currently inactive.

Chester Evans, Jr.

241 East Magnolia	San Antonio, Texas 78212
Home (512) 828-1344	Service (512) 732-6065

ESTIMATOR

Commercial Construction & Remodeling

Additions & Renovations & Modernizations

Offering five years of estimating experience for commercial projects ranging in cost from $4,000 to $75,000. Thoroughly qualified in the analysis of materials and labor costs, and in planning and scheduling the work of subcontractors.

Available immediately

TYPES OF EXPERIENCE

High-Technology Manufacturers
Restaurants & Food Service Companies
Publishers & Churches
Banks & Research Firms
City & County Government Agencies
General Business Offices

CONSTRUCTION EXPERIENCE

1987 to 1992
EVANS DESIGN & FIXTURES
EVANS CONSTRUCTION COMPANY
San Antonio & Austin

Owner and operator of two construction and remodeling firms. Complete responsibility for securing new business and maintaining profits, as well as: estimating, purchasing, job projecting, contract negotiations, subcontracting, payroll, problem solving.

Partial List of Major Clients

City of San Antonio	$30,000
Trinity Baptist Church	$18,000
National Chemsearch	$10,000
Sizzler Steak Houses	$21,000
One River Walk	$29,000
Datapoint	$18,000
San Antonio Light	$6,700
Tandy Business	$75,000
Culpepper Cleaners	$9,000
Alamo/MBank	$16,000

CONTRACTUAL REFERENCES PROVIDED UPON REQUEST

Susan Hafeli
#177 Monte Apalaches
San Juan, Puerto Rico 00926

PROFILE

Financial marketing specialist with an in-depth knowledge of corporate sales and promotion. Particularly experienced in tax-advantaged and tax-free investments.

Professional experience since 1981 has encompassed a full spectrum of public relations and advertising as an integral component in targeted marketing strategies.

Bilingual Spanish (born in Spain, now a United States citizen) and English. Proven skills in the design and production of promotional print materials. Available following a two-week notification period.

CAREER PATH

1991–Present	**Senior Account Executive**
1990–1991	**Mother & Homemaker**
1988–1990	**Account Executive**
1987–1988	**Corporate Sales Director**
1985–1987	**Account Executive**
1982–1985	**Account Executive Trainee**

EMPLOYERS
[Full-time Jobs & Freelance]

MORGAN HILL ISLAND INVESTMENTS, INC.
GRAYSON PORTFOLIO MANAGEMENT SERVICES, LTD.
TURNER-HOMES CORPORATIONS, INC.
MAJOR MARKET SURVEYS, INC.
PRINCETON INVESTMENTS CORPORATION

BIODATA

Born in Madrid, Spain, in 1956. Attended private schools in Spain and Italy. Graduate of Toledo University. Studied for two years at the Universitat von Erlangen-Nurnberg and the Goethe Institut. Freelance work while rearing young son during 1984–1985. Affiliated with many professional groups.

REFERENCES
Portfolio/Promotional Clients Upon Request

Emily Jane Hinman
14 East Third Avenue
Baltimore, Maryland 21227
(301) 439-1298

WHO I AM

A 36-year-old mother of three healthy and happy children who has managed to develop business skills while being responsible for my family's well-being.

I have a high sense of regard for the feelings, needs, and efforts of others. I'm a good problem solver with lots of common sense, and I have much enthusiasm for learning and for doing a good job.

WHAT I CAN DO

My experience has been in contrasting environments and ranges from retail sales at Kmart to serving as a volunteer case-worker (child abuse) in an impoverished neighborhood.

Some of the skills I have utilized include public relations and information gathering, money management, educational program planning, and customer service.

The essential ingredient in my successful work has been the ability to adapt quickly and effectively to changing situations, and the realization of my own limitations. I can take control or I can follow instructions.

POSSIBLE JOB APPLICATIONS

My field of interest includes retail sales and market research, office administration, or teaching.

WORK OUTSIDE THE HOME

1990 to Present

SUBSTITUTE SCHOOLTEACHER (JR. HIGH)

RETAIL SALES (SEASONAL)

RESEARCHER (DOOR-TO-DOOR)

DIRECT SALES (COSMETICS & COOKWARE)

REFERENCES ON REQUEST

Confidential Resume
SEAN O'CONNOR
(LEAVE MESSAGE: 334-2688)]

A CAREER SUMMARY

Sean O'Connor began his career in the hospitality industry in 1976 when he was attending the University of Rhode Island. After graduating with a bachelor's degree in 1980, he took the position of maître d' at the Red Rooster Tavern, a four-star restaurant housed in a historic building.

While working for this privately-owned, 130-seat restaurant, he took courses at graduate school during the morning and oversaw a 14-person staff providing formal plate service at night.

In 1983, he joined the staff of the Regency Hotel near Dulles International Airport Hotel. For the first two years he assisted the manager of the Twin Sabers restaurant, supervising a dining room and bar staff in a 255-seat penthouse restaurant.

He was promoted to Banquet Captain in 1985, with full responsibility for food quality/preparation, service, and guest satisfaction in an operation with a sales volume of $1,300,000 during 1985–1986.

At the end of 1986 he was assigned temporarily to the Penthouse Level as manager of the Twin Sabers and Whispers Disco, with an additional 16 disco employees and a $35,000 (per month) bar operation under his supervision.

In 1988, he was reassigned and promoted to Assistant Manager of the Meeting & Banquets Department; in 1990, he was promoted to his current position of Banquets Director.

His current responsibilities encompass all matters concerning banquets, conventions, and other meetings: planning, setup, and supervision (up to 1,700 guests with 100+ waiters).

In summary, his considerable expertise in managing banquets fully qualifies him to take charge of a hotel's banquet operations, and his experience would contribute significantly to a hotel's image and overall profits.

Sean offers excellent references and would be pleased to provide them along with other information in a personal interview.

Please do not contact him at his office, but leave a message at the telephone number listed above.

Name	JON A.R. PROSELL
Title	STRESS ANALYST
Current Address	2933 West Avenue Shoreline Chicago, Illinois 60666
Phone	(303) 222-8787 (303) 440-3844 Evenings (303) 440-3398
SSN	115-03-9987
Clearance	SECRET
Date of Birth	11 May 1963
Place of Birth	Denver, Colorado
Education	BSCE, Colorado University, 1983
Experience	Metallic and composite primary and secondary structural component analysis. NASTRAN FEM LTV AEROSPACE & DEFENSE CO.

3-86 to 5-88	Training program in test engineering, field service, mass properties, structures liaison, NASTRAN FEM, structures design.
5-88 to 3-90	Assigned to Corps Support Weapons System Assault Breaker Missile System. Performed stress analysis in detailed design and acceptance test phases of program.
3-90 to Present	Assigned to Advanced Development Projects Aircraft Division on the Advanced Tech Bomber Program. Contributed during conceptual through detailed design phases in critical load path development, NASTRAN FEM, internal loads generation, structural joint concept trade studies, and detailed structural component analysis. Advanced to responsible on-site stress engineer and coordinator to prime contractor for major production break interfaces on wing box and leading edge structure.

Curriculum Vitae

CHARLES W. JORGENSON

151 Cod Avenue – Boston, Massachusetts 02138 – 617/344-6690

CAREER SUMMARY

Experienced research scientist in the field of **III-V semiconductor epitaxy** and related **opto-electronic devices.**

Received M.S. and B.S. in Electrical Engineering from Cornell University with concentrated study in **optical electronics and solid state physics.**

Developed tunable UV dye laser system at NASA Drury Research Center for differential absorption LIDAR experiments. Directed development of related optical and mechanical systems by technical support staff.

Managed a **prototype crystal growth facility** at Folsom Labs for production of GaAs/A1GaAs heterojunction injection lasers. Was responsible for LPE system development, material analysis, and experimental techniques. Also studied the growth of pyro-electric materials using chemical vapor transport methods. Developed **microprocessor-controlled furnace** system to utilize gradient-reversal methods for chemical vapor transport growth.

Received Ph.D. in Electrical Engineering from Massachusetts Institute of Technology. Thesis research at MIT included the design, construction, and operation of an LPE system for growth of GaAs/A1GaAs heterojunctions; the fabrication of lasers with etched mirrors and integrated opto-electronic devices from grown material. Thesis research resulted in the development of a **monolithically integrated-single mode laser-waveguide-detector** circuit operating at .88 μm.

Developed and implemented processes leading to the large-scale production of 1.3 μm single-mode communication lasers at Northrup Labs. Was directly responsible for the subsequent technology of automated reactor design and related clean room facilities.

Presently responsible for the development of 1.3 μm and 1.55 μm single-mode communication lasers at Wheeling-Bell CSPC.

Personal attributes include rapid understanding of new technology and its application, and the organizational skills to implement new technology rapidly and efficiently; excellent verbal and written communication skills.

Barbara Hollingsworth

Bachelor of Science/Nursing   May 1992

Present Address	Permanent Address
241 Bent Branch	345 E. 27th Ave.
The Colony, Texas 75056	Denton, Texas 76205
(214) 373-2111	(817) 499-3200

EDUCATION

1988–1992   TEXAS WOMAN'S UNIVERSITY, Dallas, Texas
             Degree: BS/Nursing   Minor: Biology   GPA: 3.7

EMPLOYMENT

August 1991–   WESTGATE MEDICAL CENTER, Denton, Texas
May 1992   Part-time employment as Emergency Room Admitting
             Clerk responsible for obtaining personal data and insurance
             information from incoming patients, collecting payment
             upon patients' discharge, filling out forms per doctors'
             requests, and running errands for the nursing staff.

April 1988–   TEXAS STATE SENATE, Austin, Texas
July 1989   Senate Payroll Clerk and Senate Messenger

June 1985–   HEB FOODSTORES, Denton & Houston, Texas
May 1987   Stocker and checker during summers and holidays.

LOCATION PREFERENCE: OPEN

REFERENCES

Dr. Robert Cunningham
Professor of Nursing Research
Texas Woman's University
Dallas, Texas 76219
(214) 622-5933

Mr. Broderick A. Carnes
Emergency Room Supervisor
Westgate Medical Center
Denton, Texas
(817) 443-1988

The Honorable Joe C. Kuntz
Federal Administrative Law Judge
2600 Wagon Trail
Corpus Christi, Texas 73229
(713) 339-4988 Ext. 1775

Mr. Carlos Guerro
Former Administrative Assistant to
Texas Senate Sergeant-at-Arms
Washington, D.C.
(202) 832-6612

Eiko Nagamine
133 Kaikunane Loop #8   Honolulu, Hawaii 96817

JOB	**AGRICULTURAL MANAGEMENT**
OBJECTIVE	Farm Operations—Economic Forecasting

Seeking a position with real career potential in the field of farming or agricultural market analysis.
Available in June. Will relocate in U.S.A. or other country.

COLLEGE	**Bachelor of Science in Agricultural Economics, 1992**
EDUCATION	The University of Oregon at Portland

Minor: Business Administration   GPA: 3.4 (Overall) & 3.9 (Major)

St. John's College (Summers 1989 & 1991)
Courses: Accounting (9 Hours) & Farm Operations Management (6 Hours)

HIGH	Honors Graduate, Kananwakane Preparatory, 1988
SCHOOL	Vice President of Junior & Senior Classes
ACTIVITIES:	President of Student Council (2 Years)
	Member of Drama Club
	Member of Soccer & Volleyball Teams

MAJOR	Farm & Ranch Management (9)	Marketing (3)
COURSES &	Agricultural Economics (6)	Statistics (3)
HOURS	Agricultural Policy (3)	Business Law (3)
	Agricultural Prices (3)	Animal Science (6)
	Land Economics (3)	Farm Accounting (6)
	Government Farm Policies (3)	Crop Diseases (3)
	International Trade (3)	Business Records (3)
	Financial Planning (3)	Farm Tax Laws (3)

Special Seminars Program: "High Technology Planting" and "Modern Conservation Measures."

LANGUAGES	Some knowledge of Japanese.
WORK	Part-time jobs while attending school: art teacher in a children's school; restaurant hostess; worker in a mushroom growing greenhouse.
BIODATA	Born in Hawaii. Grew up on family-owned avocado farm.
REFERENCES	Transcripts and references upon request.

Alicia Vijil Torres
242 Bellcastle Lane
Lexington, Kentucky 40505
(502) 477-3390

DEGREES & UNIVERSITIES

| M.M. | PIANO | University of Kentucky (Lexington) | May 1992 |
| B.M. | PIANO | University of Louisville (Kentucky) | May 1989 |

HONORS & AWARDS

University of Kentucky, 1989–1992

Chosen as one of the top six accompanists in 1992.
Selected for First Place College Symphony.
Member of Phi Kappa Phi.

University of Louisville, 1986–1989.

Graduated with Highest Distinction.
Laurence C. Prescott Competition—1st Place (1989).
Amy Anderson Academic Scholarship (4 Years).
2nd Place—American Guild of Organists (1988 Competition, Lexington Chapter).
Member of Mu Phi Epsilon (Professional Music Society).
Member of Pi Kappa Lambda.

PIANO PEDAGOGY

Completed a Piano Pedagogy course for private teaching in 1990.
Taught class piano while taking a Piano Pedagogy course in 1990–1991.

TEACHING & RELATED EXPERIENCE

Private studio teaching in Kentucky and Tennessee, 1988–present.
Coach accompanist, Kentucky Ensemble & Choral Group, 1990–1991.
Accompanist/arranger, Louisville Mastersingers, 1988.

INSTRUMENTS

Training: cello and violin (4 years); harpsichord (2 years); flute.

TRANSCRIPTS FURNISHED ON REQUEST

Robert (Bobby) Reynolds
555 Hawthorne #34-A   Dallas, Texas 75211   (214) 383-3774

VIDEO PRODUCTION

Seeking an opportunity to apply formal training and hands-on experience in video production.

FCC General Radiotelephone Certificate #PG-10-6445 issued in 9/91. Age 24, married. Desire to relocate back to Minnesota. Available immediately.

FORMAL EDUCATION & ON-THE-JOB TRAINING

January 1991 to March 1992
Video Arts Technical College of Dallas

Program

40 Weeks—Electronics Technology & Troubleshooting
50 Weeks—OJT in Video Production Technology

Degree

Associate of Arts in Video Production & Technology

Graduate With Honors

Skills	Equipment
Editing	Symtec PGS with Apple IIE
Lighting	Character Graphics Generator
Set—Build/Strike	JVC KY-1900 (Camera)
Camera Operator	Sony BVU-110 (Remote Deck)
Switcher Operator	Lighting (Fresnel, Scoop
Microphones	Broad, Par 64, Leko)
Computer Graphics	Sony ECM-50
Camera—Set-Up Registration	EV Shotgun
Set Design	Sony RM-440 Editor
Directing	Oscilliscope
Floor Directing	Vectorscope
Continuity	RCU
Script Writing	Switcher & Audio Mixer
Story Development	Active Switcher
	¾" VCR
	Distribution Amp
	TBC

RELATED WORK EXPERIENCE

Private instruction in voice and guitar. Employment, 1988–Present: Woodbury Business Systems; Schmitt Music Centers; TransAmerica Film; Fotomat; Pickwick International.

BIODATA & SCHOOLS

Born in Osseo, Minnesota. Graduate of public high school (top 3rd in class of 416).

Evana Saroj

149 Sunflower	Los Angeles, California 90035	213/484-1127

Primary Goal To obtain a rewarding and responsible position where abilities, experience, and educational background in chemistry, biochemistry, and biology can be valuable.

College Education **Graduate Studies** STANFORD UNIVERSITY, 1989–1992.

Biochemical Regulations	Enzyme Biochemistry
Molecular Biology	Physical & Organic Chemistry

Undergraduate STANFORD UNIVERSITY, 1986–1989
Bachelor of Science in Chemistry; Biology minor.

Honors Graduated with a G.P.A. of 3.88/4.00
Kappa Mu Epsilon (Mathematics Honorary)
Beta Phi Omega (Biology Honorary)
3rd Place Swimmer (1988 Meet)

Work Experience: 1979 to Present

GENERAL HOSPITAL
EKG Technician 9/91–Present & 9/89–11/90

[Part-time] Record electrical impulses of patients' hearts using an electrocardiogram; read physicians' interpretations of the EKG; use computer to retrieve and input data.

TAYLOR SCHOOL OF
DENTISTRY—BIOCHEMISTRY DEPT.
Laboratory Technician 6/89–6/90

[Part- & Full-time] Assisted with faculty research projects and teaching labs of dental students; programmed quantities of department's chemicals into computer for monthly inventory.

STANFORD UNIVERSITY—CHEMISTRY DEPT. 1/87–6/88

Research Assistant, Lipid/Cholesterol Research Lab
Purified High Density Lipoprotein (HDL) subfractions and cholesterol by column chromatography and electro-fusing methods.

Teaching Assistant, Inorganic Chemistry
Prepared chemicals and pretested procedures.

Research Assistant, DNA Research Laboratory
Responsible for library research on DNA sequencing.

References *Upon request.*

Malcom R. Ridgeway
266 East Pine Circle   Mayflower Apartments #12-C
Hartford, Connecticut 39122

Objective	Entry-level opportunity at a television or radio station. Will accept any position which will provide for a long-awaited desire to work in RTF. Available now.
Colleges	The University of Connecticut at Storrs, 1992. *Graduate work: Communications* The University of Vermont at Burlington, 1989–1992. *Degree: B.A., Communications (RTF)* *Minor: Media Marketing* Kent (Ohio) State University, 1986–1987. *Major: Journalism*
Work Experience	Zale's Fine Diamonds (Storrs), 1992. **Security Guard & Courier** Radio Shack (Burlington), 1991–1992. Computer World (Burlington), 1990–1991. **Sales Assistant** Sold, delivered, and installed computers and other equipment; some telemarketing. Burlington Security Services, 1989. **Dispatcher**
Career-Related Experience	The Burlington Gazette, Summer 1991. **Copy Messenger** Received news, sports, and weather information from wire services and distributed to copy desks. Winter Sports Magazine, 1988/1990. Ski Lodge Reports, 1990–1991. **Interviewer & Layout Artist** **Delivery Supervisor** KTRH-TV Channel 12 (Kent), 1987. **Consumer Affairs Assistant** Assisted consumer advocate Marilyn Washington. Joined film crews on location and helped edit reports.
Other Activities	**KSUT-FM Radio (KSU Station)** **Co-Anchor of Talkshow** Moderated discussions/debates on live program.

Additional Details on Request

Luther ("The Poet") Maddox

12 West Lovers Lane   Before June: 492-7782
Charlotte, NC 80811   After July: 492-2659

SUMMER JOB OBJECTIVE

Children's Computer Camp Instructor

Programming & Operations

PERSONAL BACKGROUND PROFILE

Born in 1966 in North Carolina. More than ten years of active participation in competitive swimming at state and regional levels while maintaining good scholastic records. Earned 100% of educational expenses through work and scholarships. College activities also included: Forensic Team, President of Black Organizations, Editor of "College Poets" series. Own and use a personal computer (Apple) and have designed custom programs.

PHILOSOPHY

I believe that all children want to learn and need only to be encouraged with thoughtful instruction to succeed completely. I am able to communicate complex technical material in a coherent manner and I have the patience to work with children at the different paces they require. I always welcome and enjoy challenges, and I can be counted on to do a job without a lot of supervision, while I am accepting of others' considerations about my work.

COLLEGE

North Carolina Wesleyan College, *1991–[1994]*.

Transferred from Grambling State University in 1991; expect to finish curriculum in May, 1994 with a B.S. in Computer Science. I have tentative plans to attend graduate school and obtain a master's degree in computer information systems/management.

ADDITIONAL STUDIES

Completed 300+ hours of "Computer Programming for Business Applications" at DeVry Institute of Technology. Experienced with COBOL, BASIC, RPG II, and JCL. Have used, to various degrees, IBM, Commodore, Apple, and Kaypro equipment.

Interview Desired A.S.A.P.

Alani Tomi Opeloye

6821 Southwestern Drive
Las Vegas, Nevada 93021
(702) 244-8245 #309

PRIMARY OBJECTIVE

Entry-Level Position in **Mechanical Drafting** on Night Shift.
Seeking opportunity to utilize academic training and earn expenses while
attending college.

SECONDARY OBJECTIVE

To secure starting employment with a firm which is engaged in projects in
African nations. Ultimate goal is to become a project manager (hopefully) in
Nigeria.

STATUS

Expect to complete studies for a Bachelor of Science in Mechanical Engineering by the end of this summer. Will be available for full-time assignments
(U.S. or African) at that time. Willing to accept freelance work on contract
basis in the interim.

COLLEGE EDUCATION

Currently have 119 hours of coursework toward a B.S. degree.
Nevada Southern University—School of Engineering
Current Scholastic Standing: GPA 3.5 (Major), Dean's List—Four Semes-
ters
Member of American Society of Mechanical Engineers

Courses		
	Hydraulic & Pneumatic Systems	Fluid Mechanics
	Fluid Power Control	Material Science
	Nuclear Power Engineering	Metal Cutting
	Digital Systems Design	Heat Transfer
	Electro Mechanical Systems	Thermodynamics
	Optimum Mechanical Design	Synthesis (Artificial
	Synthesis of Mechanical	Intelligence Application
	Engineering Systems	of REDUCE to the
	Automatic Control, Modeling,	Engineering Discipline)
	and Analysis	Engineering Design

SUMMARY OF QUALIFICATIONS

Strong interest in computers; acquainted with BASIC and FORTRAN.
Knowledge and experience with N/C machine. Hands-on experience in designing a protective shield to prevent breakage of free-falling body. Single; no
restrictions on travel. Born in Nigeria (permanent U.S. resident).

Transcript Available from NSU Placement Office

Charles Owens   P.O.B. 2244   Austin, Texas 76539   476-2944

ELECTRONIC TECHNICIAN

Seeking a position with the potential for advancement based upon initiative and performance. Desire to use specialized military training/experience in avionics and broad knowledge of precision measuring equipment.

Available Immediately—Will Relocate Anywhere

MILITARY SERVICE: 1982–1992
Top Secret Clearance

THE UNITED STATES NAVY
Special Training Schools

10/90–4/91	**Advanced Microwave Measurement (200 HRS)**
4/90–6/90	**Advanced Electronic Measurement (150 HRS)**
6/89–11/89	**VAST Advanced Operator Controls (400 HRS)**
9/87–5/88	**Advanced Avionics (640 HRS)**
4/82–8/82	**Aviation Electronic Technician (450 HRS)**
2/82–4/82	**Basic Electricity & Electronics (180 HRS)**

NAVAL AIR STATION NORTH ISLAND: 1987–1992

CALIBRATION TECHNICIAN: Repaired and calibrated physical mechanical (torque wrenches, gages, tentiometers, inflators) and various electronic test equipment (signal generators, electronic counters, volt ohm meter, oscilloscopes). Work center supervisor and quality control inspector.

NAVAL AIR STATION MIRAMAR: 1984–1987

AUTOMATIC TEST EQUIPMENT OPERATOR. Performed and supervised lower grade personnel in the performance of maintenance on the Versatile Avionics Shop Test (VAST) and other avionics components in support of the S-3 aircraft.

NAVAL AIR STATION DALLAS: 1982–1984

AUTOMATIC TEST EQUIPMENT TECHNICIAN. Performed inspections, repairs, servicing, preventive maintenance, modifications, calibrations, removal, and replacement of parts assemblies and components in support of S-3 and F-14 aircraft. VAST operator in training.

PERFORMANCE EVALUATIONS
Copies of performance evaluations available for review on request.

Jesse Rodriquez
359 E. 50 St. #62–New York, NY 10013–(212) 432-8821

OBJECTIVE MICROWAVE SYSTEMS
REPAIR/TROUBLESHOOTING

Experience Highlights

During six years in the United States Army experience in electronics has been broad and encompassed the following duties:

  installing/repairing HF/SSB (Collins) radio systems
  alignment/maintenance of 3KW/30KW generator systems
  alignment/repair of ITT microwave systems (AN/FRC-113)
  maintaining/ordering electrical parts (PLL)
  antenna construction/repair
  pole and tower climbing

Traveled for two years throughout Germany, Belgium, and Holland repairing HF/SSB and microwave tropospheric scatter systems.

Extensive experience with test, measurement, and diagnostic equipment, including two years as Assistant Supervisor of a DCS Microwave Tropospheric Scatter Station; Commander for one year.

THE UNITED STATES ARMY: 1986–1992

Assignment **MUENSTER RADIO STATION**
1989–1992 European Defense Communications System
  DCS Microwave Station

Operated three HF/SSB Collins radios in a separate military net that operated throughout Italy, Turkey, Germany, Holland, and Belgium.

Also operated a terminal digital system (ITT) in the EDCS and two Collins SSB KWM-2A linear amplifiers and power supplies.

Assignment **DIRECT SUPPORT SHOPS**
1986–1989 Mobile Maintenance Teams (MT-V/NORGERM)

Repaired ITT microwave AN/FRC-113 and Collins SSB KWM-2A linear amplifiers and power supplies.

Worked in mobile maintenance team rush-repairing the above equipment in user locations servicing all the northern half of Germany.

Technical Electronics Training

One year: oscilloscope, frequency counter, volt meters, power meters, multimeters, db meters, tube testers, signal generators, transmission measuring sets.

Three years: microwave faults, circuit alignment, dipole repair, bench work.

Andrew Dale Raines

Call Collect Anytime: 512-732-4044

PROFESSIONAL OBJECTIVE

Position in Media/Communications with a professionally demanding staff. Looking for a company that wants a determined, hard worker.

MAJOR EXPERIENCE

Communications specialist in the United States Navy with experience in journalism, TV/radio, and recruiting. Successfully completed Navy's training programs; received achievement awards for contributions.

Journalism

Ship's on-board photographer, news writer, public affairs specialist, and minority affairs representative. Prepared news releases and public affairs materials; operated and maintained a closed-circuit TV system and photo lab.

 wrote news and feature articles for publication in local newspapers and magazines

 production manager/broadcaster for daily newscasts using a mini-cam and color slide presentations

 editor and photographer of ship's "1985 Atlantic Cruise Book" and official ship historian

 converted a stateroom into a photo lab with both B&W and color printing capabilities

Radio & TV

Radio/TV program director for a 24-hour AM-FM operation and the TV department. Supervised and trained five broadcast journalists and 16 assistants. Responsible for production management and technical functions, including taping and editing.

 organized and directed a successful 12-hour fund-raising "special" for the Navy Relief Society

Recruiting

Trained in public relations and recruiting; assigned to a two-person station in Greenville, Texas, and established a good and beneficial working rapport with civic and business leaders in the community.

 received two gold wreaths and one silver star for outstanding performance

PORTFOLIO & REVIEW TAPE AVAILABLE

Abraham John Gresham

Permanent	Current
4311 Mayport Road	106 North White
Fairfax, Virginia 22033	Altus, Oklahoma 75231
(703) 388-2145	(405) 724-8835

JOB OBJECTIVE

U.S. Air Force experience includes C-S/C1211 airframes, TF-33 power plants, and C-S wheel and tire build-ups. A&P License #427-28-3221. Available for full-time work after 20 June 1993.

UNITED STATES AIR FORCE JUNE 1986 TO JUNE 1993

Unit Aircraft Maintenance Specialist

— major maintenance on airframe components of C-141B and C-5A aircraft
— inspection, troubleshooting, removal/repair, adjustments and installation of landing gears, wing flaps, ailerons, rudders, control cables, slats, spoilers, gear boxes, and all other mechanical components
— aircraft jacking on C-141B and C-5A aircraft
— accomplishment of Time Compliance Technical Orders in accordance with prescribed directives
— responsible for ensuring timely submission of data collection for maintenance reports
— requisitioning of parts and coordination of repair and processing of aircraft and equipment components as needed

Technical Training

Aircraft Maintenance Technician (156 HRS)—May 1990.
Aircraft Maintenance Specialist (180 HRS)—June 1988.

Successfully completed four Specialized Maintenance courses (520 HRS) during 1987–1989 through Field Detachment 403.

Performance Comments

Copies Available

"His performance has been outstanding. His knowledge and ability to understand and analyze the functions of an aircraft's systems has made him one of our most highly regarded and reliable men."

[TSgt. D.L. Johnson, Commanding Supervisor]

"Gresham wants to do the best. He's exceptionally cognizant of the life-or-death ramifications of his performance. He always double-checks his work and is a fine problem solver."

[Lt. R.A. Beardsley]

Hugh Baxter
Route 7, Box 124-A   Kingsland, Texas 76159—(915) 388-5498

OBJECTIVE: COMMERCIAL PILOT—HELICOPTER

Certificates & Training	Aircraft	Flight Time
Helicopter, ATP, CFI	Beech Kingair	5,000 TOTAL
Airplane:		
single/multi-engine, land	Beech Queenair	4,475 PIC
Instrument	Beech Baron	890 Instructor
FAA Class 2 Medical	Bell 205, 206, 47G	422 Instrument
Army Pilot & Instructor Pilot		
Courses	Hiller 12D	375 Night
Aviation Safety Management		
Course	Piper 250	200 Multi-engine
	Cessna 150, 172.T-210	

PILOT OPERATIONS EXPERIENCE

Current: *Corporate Pilot: PIC in BH-206 & CE T-210.*

The United States Marines: 1979–1992

1990–1992

Aviation Safety & Standardization Officer at installation level. Wrote regulations and directives for aviation operations; organized special seminars; inspected aviation units. PIC in Bell 205 and 206 helicopters for commanders' and staff flights.

1988–1990   *Inspections Officer*

Extensive worldwide travel: established and administered written plans for operations, maintenance, safety, and training. PIC/Instructor Inspector in 205 and 206.

1987–1988

FSO developed flight regulations; administered ground, simulator, and flight instruction; conducted check rides; high-altitude mountainous terrain flights.

1981–1987   *FSO & Instructor*

Administered unit flight standardization and safety programs; transported VIPs, U.S., and foreign heads of state. Instructor for helicopter instructor qualifications course.

1979–1981

Instructed student pilots in helicopter flight school. Evaluated flight training instruction; conducted instructor pilot evaluation check rides.

Achievements	Flight Training Analysis Officer in flight school.
& Special	Selected to teach Instructor Pilot Qualification course.
Duties	Selected to fly high-level commanders and dignitaries.
	Graduated in top 10% of flight school class.
References	Civilian (corporate) references furnished at interview.

William R. Brown
(512) 489-2388

2419 New Braunfels Blvd.
San Antonio, Texas 78212

Objective   A position at the management level within a corporate
environment where fluency in Japanese and an in-depth
knowledge of Japanese culture may be of value.

Comments from U.S.A.F. Superiors

"Staff Sergeant Brown has achieved the enviable distinction of being the
almost indispensable man; he is that important to the successful accomplishment of the flight's mission . . . I had to constantly rely on his experience,
judgment, and job performance . . . he has never failed to accomplish all that
was required and more.

[Major J.T. Farnam]

"Staff Sergeant Brown distinguished himself through his keen sense of responsibility, dedication, and supervisory ability. The professional manner in
which he accomplished all tasks is indicative of his excellent growth potential."

[Colonel T.S. Scott]

"His devotion to duty and willingness to help anyone at any given moment
are but a few of his greatest assets. He has the ability to communicate with
each coworker and gain the maximum of information for final reporting. He
definitely contributes to the Equal Opportunity Program."

[Captain W.W. Wister]

"He is an exacting supervisor who instructs by example and closely monitors
the efforts of coworkers and subordinates for maximum effective performance . . . quick to recognize the potential problem areas and take immediate
action . . . thorough and without a doubt our most dependable man on the
job."

[Lt. D.S. Brown]

Experience   **THE UNITED STATES AIR FORCE: 1984–1991.**
Awarded the Air Force Commendation Medal with
Citation Clearance: TOP SECRET

*[Due to the classified nature of assignments, the following is a general and
brief outline of responsibilities.]*

In summary: seven years of supervisory experience, including research, coordination of data processing, report writing (technical), and personnel investi-
gations.

Heavy dependence upon memorization, working under strict time-pressure
schedules, and making decisions on the moment.

Education   U.S.A.F. "Supervisory Management" (140 hours).
University of Maryland extension courses at Misawa AFB,
Japan: 200+ hours, "A" average.

Personal   Age 34. Married (wife is Japanese).

Synopsis of U.S. Navy Experience
1981 to Present
MEDICAL SERVICE CORPS

Chief of Out-Patient Administrative Services

NAVAL REGIONAL MEDICAL CENTER/SAN DIEGO

Complete charge since 1988 of all administrative and clerical support services for a 460-bed general and acute medical facility, including 18 specialty clinics: Internal Medicine, Orthopedics, Psychiatry, Physical Therapy, General Surgery, Pediatrics, Emergency Room, Primary Care, Obstetrics.

Set up and directed the implementation of a special Vietnam Veterans Program to deal with the growing problem of "stress syndrome."

Prepare and manage a $1,300,000 annual operating budget for capital and operating equipment; supervise a staff of 123 military and civilian personnel; maintain all computerized (Honeywell & IBM systems) recordkeeping activities; conduct staffing and productivity studies; serve as Disaster Preparedness Control Officer.

Administrative Officer-in-Charge

NAVAL REGIONAL BRANCH CENTER

Responsible for a staff of 75 military and civilian personnel providing out-patient care for 3,300 shipyard employees and 1,800 active duty staff in shipyard and Naval support.

Administrative Resident Intern

ST. MARY'S HOSPITAL—ST. LOUIS

Completed graduate school requirements. Rotated through all administrative and clinical departments.

Commissioned as Ensign

1983—Health Care Administration Program,
Washington Univ.
1982—Health Care Planning Program, Georgia Welsey.

Education

1981—M.S. in Health Care Administration, UCLA.
1977—B.B.A. in Management, USC.

Professional Associations

ACHA *(Charter Member)*, MHA *(Board Member)*, YMCA & youth clubs.

PART FOUR

COMMON
PROBLEMS

FROM ROUGH DRAFT
TO FINAL

This section shows what can be done to improve a resume's appearance and value. The 12 before-and-after versions represent the most common problems confronting a resume writer.

Having written thousands of resumes, I have seen them in every shape and condition. One client sent out 200 resumes with "STRICKLY CONFIDENTIAL" on them, and he had never noticed his glaring misspelling. (He wondered why he wasn't getting any responses!) Another client, right out of graduate school, listed his degree as a "Master of Bussiness Administration." These errors are typical and inexcusable, and generally due to careless proofreading. And they're the sort of thing that gives a personnel manager or recruiter a good chuckle before moving on to the next applicant's resume.

A *professional resume* is simply one that has been through design-and-rewrite processes to trim off the fat and make its points sensibly. Of course, it is also typed and spaced to make it attractive and easy to read, and copied/printed on good quality paper.

Let's begin with an example of a "worst case," a resume one of my clients was using to no avail. And no wonder, because just about everything is wrong with it: format, placement and presentation of material, job descriptions, and more. A point-by-point analysis follows, showing how a skilled recruiter would pick it apart without mercy.

RESUME

> **Raymond Kelly Brown**
> *P.O. Box 2449*
> *Falcon City, Ga. 62334*
> *(218) 722-4399*
> *(713) 399-2267 (Bay City)*

POSITION

OBJECTIVE: Position leading to Management and Administrative responsibilities— Administrative Director; Personnel/Public Relations Manager; Marketing Director; Sales Manager.

SUMMARY: Highly qualified/degreed marketing professional, with background in administrative and agricultural operations with over twenty years experience. Expertise established in all aspects of supervising administrative operations. Also very proficient in sales and marketing functions; excellent public speaker, with ability to organize meetings, train personnel, and communicate ideas with all levels of management.

EDUCATION: B.B.A. Marketing Administration from Southern Methodist University (1966–1970).

MILITARY: United States Marine Corps (Oct. 1971 to Dec. 1974)—Honorably discharged with rank of Captain. Completed Officers' Candidate School, Basic Officers' School and Amphibious Track Vehicle/Armored Tank School; Served tour of duty in Vietnam as Amtrack Platoon Commander and Armored Tank Company Executive Officer; Completed military service as Company Commander of Headquarters Co. in Field Service Regiment.

EMPLOYMENT HISTORY

Equitable Life Insurance Company
Falcon City, Georgia
July 1989 to Present

LIFE INSURANCE AGENT: Engaged in marketing of Life, Health, Business Insurance, and Investments to individuals and businesses in southeast Georgia. Proficient in group health, life, disability, and retirement programs; Qualified Member of Million Dollar Round Table (1983 and 1984); Attended various seminars on sales, motivation, business insurance, and real estate/investments.

Barton Gin, Inc.
Falcon City, Georgia
July 1979 to July 1989

VICE PRESIDENT AND PRESIDENT/ MANAGER: Family Corporation consisting of 2,000-acre cotton/soybean plantation, cotton gin, liquid fertilizer dealership, and retail farm chemical/seed business. Responsible for all aspects of management and supervision, including setting up budgets and twenty personnel. Also actively involved in Georgia Cotton Producers' Association, serving as President (1983 and 1984)—represented GCPA on National Cotton Council Producer Steering Committee; Testified before U.S. Congress on 1983 Farm Bill; Appointed by Governor of Georgia in 1982 to Georgia Department of Agriculture State Market Commission.

Gulf Oil Company
Houston, Texas
Jan. 1976 to July 1979

DISTRICT SALES REPRESENTATIVE AND REAL ESTATE REPRESENTATIVE: Engaged in marketing oil products and supervising Gulf Agents and Jobbers in southeast Tennessee for 18 months. Rated top District Sales Rep. out of twenty in Houston Marketing Division. Promoted to Real Estate Representative in Houston—then responsible for disposing of old properties and acquiring new sites where performed related functions commensurate with responsibilities. Met wife in Houston during this period and left Gulf to go to work with her family in Georgia.

Army–Air Force Exchange Service
Fort Sam Houston, Texas
June, 1970 to Aug., 1971.

MANAGEMENT TRAINEE DEVELOPMENT PROGRAM: Started in training program at Fort Sill, Oklahoma, then Fort Riley, Kansas, to learn all aspects of Exchange System which included administration/personnel, retailing, warehousing, transportation, and buying. Never completed program because drafted—so joined United States Marine Corps.

PERSONAL:

Age: 47
Citizenship: U.S.
Height: 6′
Weight: 180 lbs.
Health: Excellent

Marital Status: Married: Two children—Son, age 10; daughter, age 12.

COMMUNITY INVOLVEMENT:

Board Member—Falcon City Chamber of Commerce

Secretary—Falcon City Rotary Club

Active Member—First Presbyterian Church

REFERENCES:

Excellent professional and personal references available upon request.

This resume is a complete disaster, as evidenced by the fact that Mr. Brown sent out dozens and never got so much as a "thank you" in return. No small wonder. (He also failed to use a good cover letter to introduce the resume.) The critical fault is that the resume is a jumble of data without a handle. The man doesn't seem to know where he's going. Beginning with a "shotgun" objective, he drags the hapless reader through an ill-conceived summary, adds a big chunk of Marine Corps data ("ancient history"), and then makes a muddy mire of 20 years employment. Littered with contradictions, inconsistencies, sloppy writing, and scrambled truths, it fails to say exactly what he's looking for and why he thinks he is qualified.

CRITIQUE

OBJECTIVE. He shoots too wide. Listing five titles (and implying more) leads me to think he'll take anything. It also puts the burden on me to figure out where he might be of value within my company.

SUMMARY. A lot of flag waving here that sounds like it might have been lifted verbatim from someone else's resume. Coupled with a wandering objective, these pronouncements provoke me to wonder: If this guy's so great, why is he looking for a job? Any job. His cumbersome phrases make me react this way: "highly qualified/degreed" . . . as in "pedigree?" "expertise established" . . . better have some proof. "also very proficient" . . . very? more than necessary? "excellent public speaker" . . . not if he talks like he writes.

EDUCATION. It is curious that he emphasizes a degree from two decades ago by placing it right after the summary. If he puts that much stock in it, I'm inclined to think he's starting to lose confidence in his alleged expertise. After all, how relevant could the college education be at this point? It certainly does not beef up his credentials as professed in the summary. If the degree was an M.B.A., however, I wouldn't be so picayune about the way he plays it up.

MILITARY. Now this really throws me; it's adding insult to injury. Not only is this data entirely without bearing upon his job objective and/or qualifications for corporate management/administration, personnel, public relations, marketing, or sales, but it all happened a long time ago. By positioning it here (on an almost equal basis with education), am I supposed to accept this as witness to his skills?

EMPLOYMENT. This better be good or he's lost me. I want to see some real meat, something that will support his claims. His present job is straight-up insurance sales and I presume he can verify his track record. So far OK.

The next item is where the story gets interesting. After ten years in a family-owned business he left the fold—and it doesn't look good—going from president to salesman. The description of his roles and responsibilities is confusing. I am not persuaded that he could be a viable candidate for a job within my organization.

The description of his work at Gulf is sufficiently described until he says: "met wife . . . left to go to work with her family." This is outright sabotage, and now I know how he went from sales rep to president to sales rep. The story is starting to collapse.

There's more. He continues to undermine his case by talking about events of long ago. He draws out a lengthy description of an Army–Air Force training program he did not complete, and then "confesses" to avoiding the draft by joining the Marines (a good citizen doing duty on the lam).

> **PERSONAL.** After all the waning and waxing he manages one last stroke, the discombobulated personal data which looks like a driver's permit or a weekend pass. His notation of "U.S. citizenship" is ludicrous and I wonder: What's the problem with this guy? He gives me Marines, Vietnam, the U.S. Congress, an important steering committee, a state commission and a governor, an Army–Air Force exchange service—should I think he's a Communist? And the (so-called) community involvement says nothing: It's routine duty for anyone selling fertilizer or insurance in a small southern town.

Here's how the resume should look after revising the format and rewriting the content. Remember, for the type(s) and level(s) of job(s) he is looking for, he will need individually created cover letters to aim the more general resume.

OBJECTIVE A management-level position in sales or marketing.

SUMMARY Extensive background in all aspects of sales (direct and staff management). Good "track record" of profit production; adept and well-organized administrator able to work effectively at all levels of management.

Professional Experience

1989– Present	EQUITABLE LIFE INSURANCE COMPANY Falcon City, Georgia

Agent
Sell life, health, business insurance, and investments in SE Georgia. Qualified for Million Dollar Round Table.

1979– 1989	BARTON GIN, INC. Falcon City, Georgia

General Manager
Oversaw operations of a 2,000-acre cotton/soybean farm and gin, a liquid fertilizer dealership, and a retail chemical/seed business.
Administrative responsibility for twenty personnel; prepared budgets; directed sales and marketing activities.
—President, Georgia Cotton Producers' Association
—Member, National Cotton Council Steering Committee
Appointed by the governor in 1982 to the Department of Agriculture's State Market Commission; spoke on behalf of cotton producers at U.S. congressional hearings.

Prior to 1979	GULF OIL COMPANY (Houston) Real Estate Representative (1978–1979) and District Sales Representative (1976–1979).
Education	B.B.A., Marketing, Southern Methodist University, 1970.
Personal	Age 47; married, two children; excellent health. Captain, U.S. Marine Corps, 1971–1974.
References	Upon request.

And now for the brighter side! Here's a real-life job description written by a charming young woman who would be an exemplary store manager for anyone fortunate enough to hire her. She has many fine qualities and terrific potential. If her myopic, self-centered boss had any sense he would give her the recognition she has worked so hard for. But no, blind as managers can be, he offers her no hope of professional growth or a better salary. He will watch her move on to a more promising future elsewhere, and I'd bet he'll regret it when he tries to replace her.

Her unsophisticated and down-to-earth evaluation of her responsibilities—and the subsequent depiction of her personality and management style—was a welcome relief from the usual monotoned resumes I found on my desk. I was very much tempted to just put her name and address on the write-up and leave it at that: honest, detailed, specific, inviting. However, she insisted on a more conservative approach; thus, on the finished resume:

Store Manager

Complete charge of opening a 6,000 s.f. retail store: personnel hiring/training, merchandising, customer service, inventory, advertising, problem solving.

Responsible for all financial controls: credit card and check clearances, daily deposits, sales records, and weekly reports to upper management.

Track record: the store is now one of the most profitable franchises of 15 regional outlets, with current sales volume of $160,000 monthly.

The following 12 before-and-after versions of resumes (pages 170–193) demonstrate the most common problems to be coped with. The *verso* page (left side, even-numbered) shows the problem-ridden

How I ran my store

I am very loyal. and self motivated person. I do things buy the book. - and they do change. if necessary. I am very polite and outgoing. with customers. I work as much as I need to to keep things running smoothly. (even if I am sick.) Everything I do at work. is a part of me. and I want it to show my best I always put my best forward. I know how to handle myself around others and how to handle. others. I like to work with people. and keep them happy if possible. I know when to be strong, and keep on top of employees. I am not afraid to be aggressive when necessary. I feel I would be an asset to any organization. I am also a very neat and clean. person.

-Starts -   DUTIES

I started May. 1981 - Moved out from Calif. Began as an asst mgr. To be transferred. to another store. They trained me in opening - counting money, paper. work, checking in merchandise, working with money and register, helping customers. making out schedules working with part timers and other employees.

I transferred to other store,

and started from scratch from
this was a brand new store. We
merchandised it put things where
we thought they belonged. Marked
down merch. Made customer
accommodations, handled customer
complaints, and collected on
bad checks. ~~Then the~~ then
I was promoted to manager
of another brand new store.
Hired all my own help. I
have 3 asst. mgrs. 5 part time
sales and a porter and a
security guard.

I am fully in charge of everything
Inventories-which we have every
six months. Hiring, Fireing of
employees. Any problems that
may occur. whether it be
employees arguing with customers
to a leak in the cieling,
ordering supplies -doing payroll
and keeping it at a minimum.
~~But~~ My store is busy, it is
6,000 sq. ft and grosses any
where from $10,000 to $20,000
per wk.

- Deposits
- Closing paper work
- payroll
- Book work -if we
  were off on a $8,000°°
  dollar day I would
  have to go through all
  paperwork to find it.

original; the *recto* page (right side, odd-numbered) shows the "new and improved look." Formats have been aired out and restructured for a stronger presentation, and the material has been either edited or built up to make more sense.

Readability is what we're aiming for. There is no excuse for some of the sloppiness exhibited in these (real but anonymous) examples: misspelled words, misplaced punctuation, bland and cluttered job descriptions, and vague job objectives.

Writing your own resume seems difficult partly because you have to be *objective* about yourself. It sounds tricky, but it really isn't. Who should know better than you the experience and potential you offer? We tend to get bogged down when trying to determine how the resume should look and lose our concentration on how it should sound. So, choose a hearty and attractive format, try it, and if it fits then use it. As long as the information is expressed clearly and fits the space—and you are pleased with the overall appearance—you should be able to rely on it to communicate your goals and qualifications.

Personal computers have made creating a resume much easier; they also offer more options in terms of formatting and design. Resume-writing programs, although pricey at over $50 on average, can be helpful and are available at software outlets and some bookstores. If you don't have access to a computer, or you don't know how to use one, pay someone to do it. Get it right! Remember, competition for good jobs is fierce, and resumes are a dime a dozen. It's not OK for a resume to be just OK. It has to stand out and do the best job.

A resume should look like a resume, not an application form. It should need no identification tag at the top, such as "Resume" or "Personal Resume Of." If it's not immediately manifest in appearance, either the writer has failed miserably or the reader is helplessly uninformed.

Copies should be made from a spotless original—the master—which should be kept safe and clean for later use. If you've stored your resume on a computer disk, always back up the file on your hard drive or on another disk. (Starting from scratch the second time is really a drag.) The paper you use to print/copy on should be of good quality and fairly conservative in color: white, beige, light gray/blue are acceptable. Colored ink is usually more expensive and an unnecessary frill. Don't get too fancy; keep it clean and simple. (I saw a company that offers to print your name in large gold letters on the resume—for a sizable charge—as if this would really show what you're worth.)

In the examples the specific career/job objectives are irrelevant for the purposes of this section. The format used for an automobile salesman can be used just as well by a chemical engineer or law enforcement official. The formats presented are standard and lend themselves to most situations. If your resume absolutely won't fit on one page, then the second page must follow the format established on the first.

Here are some basic rules for writing, designing, and typing the final version from the rough draft.

1. Leave plenty of white space: at least 1″ margin on both sides (readers like this

for making comments) and ¾″ on top and bottom. Add extra space between major data categories.

2. If possible, use a word processing program and computer printer that can accommodate several type styles and sizes. Use a smaller font size when space is tight; larger when you need to fill out the otherwise skimpy page.

3. Be consistent. If you underline one title, underline all; if you abbreviate one city, abbreviate all. Stay in line with established indentations.

4. First things first: Job objectives and summaries go before experience and education, and everything else follows.

5. Tie down objectives and make them understandable. The resume should make sense even if separated from the embellishing cover letter.

6. Summaries: concise, confident, factual, to the point, and modest while reasonably affirmative. Edit down to the primary considerations.

7. Experience: Titles and job descriptions reign, dates are secondary, employers' addresses unnecessary. Delineate major responsibilities from secondary functions. Control chronology.

8. Education: only the relevant and recent. Be ready to show documentation.

9. *Proofread! Proofread! Proofread!* Check everything, every word. Have a

friend or two proofread for typograph-
ical or spelling errors (which tend to slip
by in names and addresses). Double-
check dates for accuracy and consist-
ency.

Original

Personal Resume

Applicant:	Donald Richard Arnheimer, Jr.
Address:	2257 Featherbrook Road
	Cuyahoga Falls, Ohio 44221
	266-8834

CAREER OBJECTIVE:

To secure a challenging engineering technician position with the opportunity for advancement.

PERSONAL DATA

Date of Birth:	6-15-68
Height:	6'
Weight:	185
Marital Status:	Single
Health:	Excellent

EDUCATION:

Garfield High School
Akron, Ohio 44301
Graduated: 6/86
Vocational Electronics (2 years)

University of Akron
Akron, Ohio 44304
Basic Electronics I (non-credit)

United Electronics Institute
Cuyahoga Falls, Ohio 44221
Graduated: 4/88
Electronics Technology

9900 Microprocessor Training
Sponsor: DataCom, Inc.
(two-40 hour classes)

EXPERIENCE:

DataCom, Inc.
P.O. 66344

Full-Time—Technician
92-12-90 to present
Reference: Mr. David South

Duties: Lead Technician—testing everything from analog and digital circuits to mechanical sub-assemblies. Other responsibilities include interfacing with engineering and production control. In addition, I have experience with 960/990 based Automated Test Stations.

Revised

Donald Richard Arnheimer
2257 Featherbrook Road
Cuyahoga Falls, Ohio 44221
Home Telephone: 266-8834

Job Objective **ENGINEERING TECHNICIAN**

Qualifications Experienced lead technician with supplementary specialized training.

Accustomed to the pressures of tight deadlines and overtime work. Able to learn new bench techniques in different environments.

Technical Work Experience DataCom, Incorporated
Post Office Box 663449
Cleveland, Ohio 43422

Lead Technician: 2/90—Present
Sub-Assembly Division

Responsible for testing a wide range of DC products from analog and digital circuits to mechanical sub-assemblies.

Frequent interfacing with personnel from engineering, production, and quality control.

In addition, have some experience with the 960 and 990 based Automated Test Stations.

Special Training Completed two 40-hour classes on "9900 Microprocessor" sponsored by DataCom.

Diploma in Electronics Technology, 1988.
United Electronics Institute
Cuyahoga Falls, Ohio

Completed "Basic Electronics" course at University of Akron, Ohio.
Diploma in Vocational Electronics (2-year program), Garfield High School (Akron).

Personal Data Born in 1968. Single. Excellent health.

References Upon request.

Original

Personal Resume

GREGORY THOMAS 2660 Falcon Drive Garland, TX 75042 (214) 433-8988

Birthdate: September 10, 1966

Work Experience:

May 1984– Sept. 1986:	**Turfs of Texas**—Hydro-mulching of lawns and preparation and finishi of same lawns. Company went out of business. Salary: $2.00/hr.–$3.00/hr.
May 1987– May 1988:	**Homer's Home Center**—1844 Promenade Shopping Center. Richardson, TX. 214-3391. Lumber sales and stocking of lumber products. Changed jobs to begin auto parts sales. Salary: $2.62/hr–$3.00/hr.
May 1988– June 1989:	**SouthFork Ford**—13442 N. Central Expwy. Dallas, TX 344-2988. Auto parts sales. Company went out of business. Beginning salary: $3.00/hr. Ending salary: $700 month base pay plus commission. Commission averaged $1,000/month.
Oct. 1989– July 1991:	**Regency Lincoln & Mercury**—Lemmon and Thorpe. Dallas, TX 357-3340. Auto parts sales. Salary: $800 month base pay plus commission. Commission averaged $1,000/month.
July 1991– Present:	**North Central Chevrolet**—1225 N. Central Expwy. Richardson, TX 231-1145. Auto parts sales. Salary: $800 month base pay plus commission. Commission averages $1,200/month.

Personal References:

Jerry Donaldson
P.O. Box 225
Princeton, TX 75077
(214) 722-8823

Mr. & Mrs. Raymond Belknap
411 Cowden Lane
Richardson, TX 75080
(214) 522-8854

Mr. & Mrs. Joe Maddox
244 Paisley Place
Richardson, TX 75080
(214) 235-8829

Revised

Gregory Thomas
2660 Falcon Drive
Garland, Texas 75042
(214) 433-8988

Job Objective   Sales position with a local automobile dealer.

Qualifications   Offering four years of automobile parts sales experience
with major dealers. Possess a full knowledge of financing
arrangements and all other facets of closing a sale.

Track Record   One of the top five profit producers at current
dealership. Consistently over quota.

Sales Experience

July 1991–   **North Central Chevrolet**
Present   *Location: North Central Expressway Richardson, Texas*

Automobile and parts sales at the highest volume
location of four owned by the dealer.

Oct. 1989–   **Regency Lincoln & Mercury**
July 1991   *Location: Lemmon & Thorpe Dallas, Texas*

Automobile parts sales and acting parts department
manager on occasion. Earned largest sales commissions
of sales staff during last three months of employment.

May 1988–   **SouthFork Ford**
June 1989   *Location: North Central Expressway Dallas, Texas*

Gained first experience in automobile and parts sales.
Prior to the company's bankruptcy, earned excellent
commissions.

REFERENCES   *Local references furnished upon request.*

Original

ROBERT L. WARNER
324 MT. View Dr. Hartsfield, AL 35640
205/445-1988

Marital Status: Married
Children: Two Girls
Health: Excellent

Education

College: Southern Illinois University, Carbondale, IL
Graduated: August, 1979
Major: Chemistry **Minor:** Mathematics
Grades: B average

Work Experience

2/91–Pres. **Employer:** Jones Blair Co, Hartsfield, AL
Position: Technical Manager, Industrial Coatings
Division
Supervisor: Allan Gunther, Division Supervisor

Responsibilities: Management of technical support to maintain and build on industrial coatings business in heavy duty maintenance and product finishes, zinc rich primers, epoxies, acrylics, urethanes, polyesters, alkyds, air dry and bake, conventional, high solids and waterborne. Supervision of four chemists and four technicians.

3/87–2/91 **Employer:** Whittaker Coatings, Decatur, AL
Position: Group Leader, General Industrial Coatings
Supervisor: Bob Wells, Business Manager

Responsibilities: Development of high solids, waterborne and conventional product finishes including alkyds, polyesters, epoxies, acrylics, and silicones. End uses were aluminum extrusions, appliances, metal furnature, wood stoves and general metal finishing. All quality control, production support and rework for general industrial products as well as field service work. Supervision of one chemist and three lab. technicians.

2/81–9/86 **Employer:** The Sherwin-Williams Co, Chicago, IL
Position: Chemist, Appliances & Extrusions Group
Supervisor: Dan Wilson, Section Supervisor

Responsibilities: Development of high solids and conventional coatings and assistance with production and field problems.

9/79–12/80 **Employer:** Standard T Chemical, Chicago Heights, IL
Position: Lab. Technician, Electrodeposition Group
Supervisor: Bill Munson, Group Leader

Responsibilities: Development of coatings for electro-deposition. Worked full-time during breaks and summers.

Interests: Fishing, Skiing, Boating, Camping, Family

Revised

Robert L. Warner
324 Mountain View Drive
Hartsfield, Alabama 35640
(205) 445-1988

SUMMARY OF QUALIFICATIONS

Technical manager with in-depth experience and expertise in the development of industrial coatings and product finishes.

Strong background in quality control, supervision of laboratory technicians, and production management.

Bachelor of Science in Chemistry, Southern Illinois University, Carbondale, Illinois, 1979.

PRODUCTION EXPERIENCE

JONES BLAIR COMPANY
1991 to Present Hartsfield, Alabama
Technical Manager, Industrial Coatings Division

Responsible for the management of technical support to maintain and build on industrial coatings business in heavy duty maintenance and product finishes, zinc rich primers, epoxies, acrylics, urethanes, polyesters, alkyds, air dry and bake, conventional, high solids, and waterborne. Supervise four chemists and four technicians.

WHITTAKER COATINGS, INCORPORATED
1987 to 1991 Decatur, Alabama
Group Leader, General Industrial Coatings

Led the development of high solids, waterborne and conventional product finishes, including: alkyds, polyesters, epoxies, acrylics, and silicones. End uses: aluminum extrusions, appliances, metal furniture, wood stoves, and general metal finishing.
Responsible for all quality control, production support, and rework for general industrial products and field servicing. Supervised one chemist and three laboratory technicians.

SHERWIN-WILLIAMS COMPANY
1981 to 1986 Chicago, Illinois
Chemist, Appliances & Extrusions Group

Developed high solids and conventional coatings: assisted with production and field problems.

PERSONAL

Married, two children. Interests: fishing, skiing, boating, camping.

Original

Joyce Denice Baylor
2755 South Baltimore   Chicago, Illinois 60517   (312) 475-8823

Job Objective:

I am seeking a position which I can fully utilize my special skills, education, and work experiences within a company that will allow for advancement and growth.

Education

CHICAGO STATE UNIVERSITY
Bachelor of Science in Mathematics-Secondary Ed.
State of Illinois Certification—April 1989

Curriculum included:

Fortran I   Fortran II   Linear Programming—325

Summary of Qualifications

3-½ years of teaching experiences:

a) 1 year of high school math;

b) 3 college semesters of business courses;

c) 2 years of advanced typewriting in adult education: and

d) 16 weeks of Business English and spelling.

Coordinated the initial states of the General Services Administration (GSA) Project—entering data of (federal government) landowners titles and codes on the Xerox 820.

Supervised a cross-training study of college students on the Xerox Word Star.

Counseled adults in resume writing.

Designed and developed the student, instructor and lab class schedules.

Work Experiences

10/90 to present **Washington Business Institute**—Chicago
Instructor/Counselor—Advanced Typewriting, Business English, and Spelling.

6/87 to 6/90 **Unity High School**
Mathematics Instructor/Freshmen Moderator—Algebra I (Honors), Algebra II, and General Business Math.

Personal Data:

Age 36. Three children. Married. Excellent health.

References:

Will be furnished on request.

Revised

Joyce Denice Baylor
2755 South Baltimore   Chicago, Illinois 60517   (312) 475-8823

Career Goal	OFFICE ADMINISTRATION: *Secretarial or related administrative position with long-term career potential.*
Professional Skills	Skilled in organizing work plans and activities for groups and individuals.
	Accomplished instructor with the ability to supervise and coordinate special studies.
	Able to cope with the details of government projects while assuring progress of daily work.
	Experienced in the use of personal computers; able to use FORTRAN and linear programming.
Experience Profile	INSTRUCTOR & PROJECT COORDINATOR *Business Institute & Public High School* 3½ years of full-time teaching, including: college business courses; adult education (English and spelling); high school mathematics. supervised a cross-training study of college students for Xerox Corporation coordinated initial stages of the General Services Administration project designed and developed student, instructor and lab class curriculums and schedules
Employers	Washington Business Institute, 1990–Present. Chicago, Illinois
	Unity High School, 1987–1990. Chicago, Illinois
Education	Bachelor of Science in Mathematics, 1989. Chicago State University
	State of Illinois Secondary Education Certification
References	Upon request.

Original

William A. Ridgestone
104 Walker Ave., Arlington, Texas 76012, Home (817) 499-2388

Objective

Seeking a challenging and responsible assignment in the FOOD SERVICE INDUSTRY where management skills, experience and proven abilities will have valuable application toward continued professional advancement.

Summary of Experience

Background encompasses over 20 years successful experience in the field resulting in expertise in the following areas:

Personnel Selection . . . Training . . . Supervision . . . Scheduling . . . Evaluation . . . Payroll Administration

Distribution Coordination . . . Purchasing . . . Transport . . . Inventory Control . . . Cost Analysis . . . Supply Expediting . . . Contract Negotiations . . . Shipping & Receiving

Sales and Marketing . . . Advertising . . . Promotional Campaign Design . . . Customer Service . . . Account Service . . . Product Presentation . . . Proposal Preparation

Administration . . . Negotiation of Franchise Contracts . . . Report Preparation . . . Financial Analysis . . . Long-Range Planning . . . Profit and Loss Responsibility

Facility Management . . . Creation of Local Supply Sources Staffing . . . Facility Layout . . . Maintenance Scheduling . . . Purchase of Capital Equipment . . . On-Site Supervision of Construction

Strengths

Possess "hands-on" operational skills . . . very proficient in this area.

Capable of meeting day-to-day objective while attaining long-range goals.

Analytical . . . proficient at assessing operations and offering/implementing cost-saving recommendations.

Personable . . . easily establishes and maintains productive relationships with all types of people.

Experience

Current	Cowboy Bill's BBQ Franchisee, Arlington, TX
	Operations Director
1988–1991	Self-employed, Tulsa, OK
	Opened own restaurant. Due to economic reasons could not expand into multi-unit operation, therefore sold the restaurant.
1981–1988	Bag 'n Bottle, Inc.
	Supervisor
	Traveled throughout the network of facilities and inspected physical location, management policies, inventory/sales figures.
Availability	Pending current notification. Will travel and/or relocate.

Revised
See Letter on Page 214

William A. Ridgestone
104 Walker Avenue, Arlington, Texas 76012, Phone 817/499-2388

Objective	A challenging position in the FOOD SERVICE INDUSTRY where proven abilities in management may be fully utilized. Will travel/relocate.
Profile of Strengths	Possess the hands-on operational skills to get the job done proficiently. Adept in analyzing problems and evaluating operations. Ability to manage daily work without losing focus on long-term objectives. Able to establish and maintain productive relationships with people of all types.
Experience Overview	Professional background encompasses twenty years of experience in the food service industry.

Personnel: selection, training, supervision, evaluation.

Distribution: coordination, purchasing, transportation, inventory control, cost analysis, supply expediting.

Marketing: advertising plans, promotional campaign design, account services, proposal preparation, product presentations, point-of-sale studies, customer service.

Sales Administration: negotiation of franchise contracts, report preparation, financial analyses, short- and long-range planning, budgeting, profit and loss responsibility.

Facility Management: creation of local supply sources staffing, facility planning and layout, location evaluation, maintenance scheduling, improvements and refurbishing, purchase of capital equipment, and onsite supervision of construction.

Experience	Current

Operations Director, *Cowboy Bill's BBQ Franchise Arlington, Texas*

1988 to 1991
Self-employed Restaurant Owner, *Tulsa, Oklahoma*

1981 to 1988
Operations Supervisor, *Bag 'N Bottle, Incorporated Home Office: Oklahoma City*

References	*Upon request.*

Original

L. Byron Shubert
5614 West Trout   New Orleans, Louisiana 70126   (504) 445-1299

Objective:	Management Related Position, *in engineering or manufacturing, with a strong office automation firm in the Portland, Oregon area.*
Education:	
4–92	Tulane University of Louisiana *Master of Business Administration*
12-88	Gonzaga University, Spokane, Washington *Bachelor of Science in Mechanical Engineering*
Other:	General Dynamics: Supervisor training (40 hrs.), *Juran Training (48 hrs.), and Carrier HVAC Class*
Experience:	
1-89 to present	General Dynamics, New Orleans, Louisiana *Corporate Services Division*
10-91 to present	**Engineering Section Manager** leading eight to twelve project coordinators and design engineers in one million square foot complex's facilities engineering department. Responsible for expenditures of $2.7 million in 1985 that included a variety of capital projects, such as: Hi-Purity Process Gas Distribution System for entire building, new Ion Implant Clean Room, and design of new Photomask Zero Defects Clean Room.
10-90 to 10-91	**Project Coordinator** for design and construction of new Class 10 Clean Room ($2 million project completed on schedule and within budget).
1-89 to 10-90	**Mechanical Engineering Design** concentrating primarily on providing building manufacturing groups with utilities needed for their equipment and production environments.
Summers 1986 and 1987	Kaiser Aluminum and Chemical Corporation Trentwood, Washington *Maintenance Engineer (in training)*
4-80 to 6-85	Boise Cascade Corporation, Kettle Falls, Washington Five years in plant maintenance department; last eight months as construction supervisor. First sixteen months as production laborer.
References:	References will be furnished on request. Please do not contact present employer until a mutual interest has been established.

Revised
See Letter on Page 213

Confidential

L. BYRON SHUBERT
5624 West Trout   New Orleans, Louisiana 70126   (504) 445-1299

MANUFACTURING MANAGER

Manufacturing engineer with five years of managerial experience encompassing proactive and reactive problem solving, functional group supervision, and cost control.

Professional Experience

GENERAL DYNAMICS   1989 TO PRESENT

CORPORATE SERVICES DIVISION

ENGINEERING SECTION MANAGER: 1991–Present.

In charge of 8–12 project coordinators and design engineers in 1,000,000 sf complex's Facilities Engineering Department.
Responsible for expenditures of $2,700,000 in FY1986 that included a variety of projects, such as: Hi-Purity Process Gas Distribution System for the entire building, a new Ion Implant Clean Room, and the design of a new Photomask Zero Defects Clean Room.

PROJECT COORDINATOR (1990–1991) for the design and construction of a new Class 10 Clean Room ($2,000,000 project) that was completed on schedule and within budget.

MECHANICAL ENGINEERING DESIGNER (1989–1990) concentrating primarily on providing building manufacturing groups with utilities needed for their equipment and production environments.

Experience Prior to 1989

Kaiser Aluminum & Chemical Corp., Trentwood, Wash. Maintenance engineer in training: summers 1986–1987.

Formal Education

M.B.A., Tulane University of Louisiana, 1992.
B.S., Mechanical Engineering, Gonzaga University, 1988.
Juran Training, General Dynamics (48 hours), 1991.

REFERENCES UPON REQUEST

Please do not contact present employer until mutual interest has been established.

Original

Ronald Smith
Box 4-A, Route 15
Karnes City, Iowa 44329

Applying for Position Of: Construction Superintendent

Positions Held:
Construction Superintendent
D & D Construction, Raytown, Iowa 1974–75
I coordinated subcontractors, ordered materials and hired personnel. I scheduled the job to expediate it to completion.

Carpenter
H.H. Kateson Construction Company, Dallas, Texas, 1990. Construction of high rise buildings.

General Contractor
R.A. SmithnConstruction Company, Karnes City, Iowa
As a general contractor, I constructed metal buildings, churches, gasoline service stations, car washes and residential homes. In these jobs, I did the estimating, letting contracts to subcontractors, carpentry work and scheduling. On the homes, I did the concrete work, plumbing, wiring, furnace installation, sheet rock taping and bedding, painting, interior trim and tile setting.

Education:
Basic Computer Course 1988
Long View College, Iowa City, Iowa

Brokerage Course 1976
Weaver Real Estate School, Iowa City, Iowa

Military Service—Army, 1958–60

Pleasant Hill High School
Pleasant Hill, Missouri
Graduated 1956

Organizations:
Karnes City Jaycees
Lions Club

Masonic Lodge
Scottish Rite
Shrine

Personal: Single, born September 19, 1940
            Four children
            Height: 5'8" Weight: 195 lbs.

Revised

Ronald Smith
Box 4-A, Route 15
Karnes City, Iowa 44329

CONSTRUCTION SUPERINTENDENT

FOREMAN & PROJECT MANAGER—GENERAL CONTRACTOR

Offering more than twenty years of experience in every facet of commercial
and residential construction and renovation.

Expertise developed in all major construction functions from planning stages
through finish-out and architect's and city agency inspections.

Project Management
Estimating & Subcontracting
HVAC & Electrical
Residential & Commercial Plumbing
Excavation & Slab Foundations

Accustomed to supervising and scheduling work crews (up to 150 workers)
and organizing work flow to meet schedules.

Projects
Shopping Centers & Churches
Medical Buildings
Office & Apartment Complexes
Warehouses & Gas Stations
Swimming Pools & Greenhouses

Employment History

General Contractor since 1981 in Karnes City. Constructed metal buildings,
churches, gas stations, car washes, and custom homes. Responsible for all
estimating, negotiations with subcontractors, scheduling, and materials
planning.

In charge of all concrete work, plumbing, wiring, HVAC, sheet rock taping
and bedding, painting (interior and exterior), tile setting, and furnace installation.

Trade References Furnished on Request

Original

Resume of:
Edward Gregg Wyman III
345 Rosewood Avenue #48-C
Greensboro, North Carolina 28210   Telephone: 704-245-8845

Occupation Objective:

Sales management position with mid-sized or large manufacturer or distributor. A position that offers potential and challenge to reach top sales and management levels.

Experience Highlights:

1985–present   KLL. Industries, Inc.
                            One retail store specializing in home furnishings.

President

KLL was formed in Aug. 1989 to expand and relocate existing operation called Designer Sleeper and Sofa Store which I (Ed Wyman) owned and operated from 1988. Further information available on request.

1985–1988   Wyman And Associates, Wholesale furniture
                         manufacturing representative, Territories: North
                         Carolina and Kentucky.

Responsibilities:

Develop and manage new territory Build sales by calls on customers, Retail Stores, contractors, and Interior Designers. Participating in all Trade Shows.

1982–1985   The Building Story, Inc.
                         Five retail furniture stores, specializing in designer home
                         furnishings. $2.8 million in 1985

Sales and operations Manager

Coordinated expansion to multiple locations. Supervised, trained and motivated management and sales personnel. Monitored inventory control and distribution. Assisted in buying and merchandising all lines of goods.

Education: Thomas Jefferson High School, Charlotte, North Carolina.

Early Background: Grew up in Charlotte. Father is a sales representative; Mother is a housewife. Have two older brothers, one younger. Attended a parochial grade school and raised in the Catholic religion.

Military Service: No obligation.

Business Interests: Marketing.

Salary: Open to negotiations.

References: Personal references available on request.

Revised

Edward Gregg Wyman III
345 Rosewood Ave. #48-C   Greensboro, NC 28210   (704) 245-8845

Objective	A position in sales management with a manufacturer or distributor where more than 10 years of successful experience may be of the greatest value.
Experience Highlights	Strong background in marketing of products in new territories. Effective administrator of sales staff and able to train/motivate for tough competition. Skilled in solving distribution network problems and related inventory control factors.

Employment History

1985–Present	KLL Industries/Wyman & Associates, Inc.
	Greensboro, North Carolina
	General Manager, KLL Industries
	As G.M. of KLL since 1989, responsible for all aspects of daily operations, including sales staff management, new location financing and on-site set-up, marketing plans, and overall profit/loss analysis.
	Note: KLL is a family-owned business that manufactures and distributes designer sleeper-sofas in the Southeast and Atlantic Seaboard markets.
	Director, Wyman & Associates, Inc.
	Fayetteville, North Carolina
	Co-owner and managing director of a business representing wholesale manufacturers. Territory: North Carolina and Kentucky.
	Operated this company independently from 1985 to 1989, with complete responsibility for marketing and sales. Company was reorganized and merged with KLL Industries in 1989.
1982–1985	The Building Story, Inc.
	Fayetteville, North Carolina
	Sales & Operations Manager
	In charge of all operations of this retail furniture chain (5 outlets) specializing in designer home furnishings. Coordinated expansion to multiple locations; hired, trained, motivated, and supervised additional sales personnel; bought and merchandised all lines; monitored inventory control and distribution.
References	*Provided upon request.*

Original

NAME	: MIGUEL B. FORBRADA
ADDRESS	: 4200 Northgate Blvd Apt 377
Indianapolis Ind.	

OBJECTIVE
: Personnel Director
Industrial and Public Relations
Purchasing Manager
Junior Executive
For a few years my experience has covered a
diversified area including Personnel, Payroll,
Management, Salary and Wages, Public
Relations, Industrial Relations, Purchasing and
Hospital Operating Rooms.

SPECIALIZED
CAPABILITIES
: Ability to execute at management level.
Professionally and socially well acquainted.
Able an capable to deal with people.
Capable to motivate them and develop their
talents to their maximum potential.
Responsible for the direct supervision of 86
females in their jobs.

OF SPECIAL INTEREST : Own a car and a house.
Have traveled extensively throughout the
United States and Puerto Rico.

EDUCATION
: Catholic University of Puerto Rico, Ponce.
Bachelor Degree in Business Administration.
Major in Management

BUSINESS HISTORY
: From 1990 to 1992,
Company: Hospital Matilde Brenes, Inc.
Position: Personnel Director
From 1984 to 1990,
Company: Damas Hospital
Position: Operating Room Manager

In charge of all personnel aspects in the Hospital.
President of Activities Committee (social).

As Operating Room Manager in charge of 62
persons including R.N., L.P.N., O.R. Technicians, Secretaries, Office Clerk, Recovery
Room Personnel and Escolts. Being and administrative, in all personnel aspects, purchases,
equipment, security, posting of cases, charges
to patients, interviewing salesmen, dealing with
doctors, patients, public in general, nurses,
dealing with the two Unions, etc.

As Personnel Director and being the second in
command in the Hospital, in charge of all personnel aspects.

Revised

Miguel B. Forbrada
4200 Northgate Boulevard   Apartment 377
Indianapolis, Indiana 44320

POSITIONS	**Personnel Director**
HELD	*Hospital Administrative Offices*
	Industrial & Public Relations Director
	Purchasing Manager
AREAS OF	Personnel Administration; Payroll; Salary & Wage
EXPERIENCE	Administration; Industrial Relations; Public Relations;
	Purchasing; Inventory Management; Supplier Contracts
	Analysis; Staff Reorganization; Pension Fund Investments;
	Benefits Plans.
PERSONAL	Fluent Spanish/English. Able to deal effectively with
PROFILE	people and to develop their talents to their maximum
	potential. Skillful problem solver and negotiator with a
	reputation for being fair and considerate of others' needs.
EDUCATION	Bachelor of Business Administration in Management.
	Catholic University of Puerto Rico at Ponce.
EMPLOYMENT	Hospital Matilde Brenes, Inc., 1990–1992.
	Ponce, Puerto Rico
	Personnel Director

Responsible for all administrative functions concerning 138 personnel (full-time salaried and part-time hourly), including department managers and shift supervisors.

In addition, served on numerous committees with responsibility for planning of public relations programs, revamping of wage structure, purchase of new diagnostic equipment, and retraining of lab technicians.

Damas Hospital
Ponce, Puerto Rico
Manager, Operating Room Services

In charge of 62 personnel, including R.N., L.P.N., O.R. technicians, Recovery Room personnel, and secretaries. Purchased supplies and equipment; scheduled/posted cases; supervised accounting of charges to patients; dealt with two local unions.

Original

Resume

Willard J. Wilson   5009 Parker Lane   Cincinnati, Ohio 34559
Phone: (513) 344-7848

Birth: 8/20/51   Health: Excellent

Work Experience	RTA Electric Supply Co.	6/7/90–5/3/92
	4533 Reading Road	Truck Driver
	Cincinnati, Ohio	Warehouse Fork Lift
	(513) 242-7700	Operator
	Able Express	10/1/89–5/20/90
	2170 Buck Street	Sales, Service
	Cincinnati, Ohio	Customer Relations
		Truck Driver
	Columbus Parcel Service	7/7/87–12/1/88
		Driver Supervisor
		Coordination of all
	Priority	freight.

Education: **University of Cincinnati—1981–1986**

College of Community Services
Major: Sociology, Minor: Psychology
Grade Average: 3.4—Dean's List
Volunteer Work—Coordinated with University
Studies: Juvenile Probation/Counseling of Alcoholics
and Veterans
Day Care Center for Underprivileged Children

Military Service: United States Army: 10/11/68–7/15/71
Honorable Discharge
Certificate of Completion—U.S. Army
Transportation School
Graduated—3rd of 187
Republic of Vietnam: 2/5/69–7/2/71
National Defense Service Medal
Vietnam—Service Medal, Campaign Medal
Army Commendation Medal, Army Medal for Valor
Vietnam Cross of Gallantry

References: Personal and Business available upon request.

Revised

Willard J. Wilson
5009 Parker Lane   Cincinnati, Ohio 34559
Phone: (513) 344-7848

JOB OBJECTIVE

Entry-level position in sales offering a chance to demonstrate initiative and abilities. Willing to put in the hard work and long hours to get the job done.

SYNOPSIS

Vietnam veteran with more than three years of college studies. (A bachelor's degree is expected to be awarded within the next six months.) Active in volunteer programs. Enthusiastic and outgoing individual who enjoys challenging tasks and likes to do the best job. Quick learner with patience.

WORK EXPERIENCE

RTA Electric Supply Co.	6/90–5/92
Cincinnati, Ohio	Warehouse Worker
(513) 242-7700	Truck Driver
	Fork Lift Operator
Able Express	10/89–5/90
Cincinnati, Ohio	Salesman
(513) 388-4262	Truck driver
	Service Rep.
Priority Dispatch	7/87–12/88
Cincinnati, Ohio	Driver supervisor
(513) 388-3299	Freight Coordinator

COLLEGE EDUCATION

University of Cincinnati, 1981–1986 & 1991–Present.
College of Community Services
Major: *Sociology* **Minor:** *Psychology*
Grade Point Average: 3.4 (Dean's List)
Volunteer Work
Counselor: Juvenile Probation; Vietnam Veterans; Alcoholics. Recreation leader at a day care center for underprivileged children.

MILITARY SERVICE

United States Army, 1968–1971.
Completed Transportation School (3rd of 187).
Vietnam tour of duty: 2/5/69–7/2/71.
Numerous commendation medals; honorable discharge.

REFERENCES

Transcripts and references furnished on request.

Original

Elizabeth Johnson   **Resume**
1088 Magnolia Road
Boston, Massachusetts 02138   Telephone: (617) 422-2766

Objective	Seeking a challenging position in the Marketing Management area of business which offers opportunity for growth, contribution and advancement.
Employment Feb. 1992 to Present	Medco Laboratory Services (MLS), Boston, Massachusetts **Coordinator/Manager**

As coordinator, responsible for the planning, implementation, and execution of all Medco operations, market development and delivery of quality services to insurance companies and their clients.

Specific responsibilities include:

a. Supervisory—Recruit, interview, and select field employees; communicate with in-office personnel as well as reviewing channels of communication with home-office, agents and mobile examiners.

Additional duties include reviewing Medco work areas to assure that proper forms and procedures are utilized to minimize time and error; and to assist, when necessary, with Colesberg operations.

b. Administrative—Receive and fill agents orders and requests quickly and effectively; Follow through with agents to assure serviceability by keeping agents informed to appointments, problems, and completions; also maintain current records and submit required reports on a timely basis.

c. Managerial—Train, coordinate and motivate staff personnel; handle problems promptly and effectively and continually evaluate progress toward goals.

d. Marketing—Introduce Medco programs and services prospective clients; develop and maintain rapporte with insurance agents; develop marketing plans, goals, and objectives and to assure regular follow-through.

e. Public Relations—Involved with local and national association for Life Underwriters; assist home office in obtaining approval to service new insurance companies.

f. Medical—Perform examinations in office an in field; keep equipment maintained and insure that medical information is accurate; and keep all supplies readily available to the examiners.

Jan. 1990 to Dec. 1991	Boston Memorial Hospital, Boston, Massachusetts Phlebotomy Supervisor

Responsible for all procedures performed in phlebotomy section including distribution of job assignments and requisition of help as needed. Also, responsible for inventory.

Education	B.S., Marketing (major), Boston College, 1990.
Personal Data	Age 28. Divorced, no children.

Revised

Elizabeth Johnson

1088 Magnolia Road   Telephone:
Boston, Mass. 02138   (617) 422-2766

Objective	Marketing Management
Employment	*February 1992 to Present* **MANAGER & COORDINATOR** Medco Laboratory Services (MLS), Boston, Mass. As manager and coordinator of the diversified services offered by MLS, responsible for planning, implementing, and executing of marketing programs to insurance companies and their clients.
Supervision:	Recruit, interview, and select field employees; review channels of communication with home office, agents, and mobile examiners; review work areas to assure proper forms and procedures are utilized.
Administration:	Receive and fill agents orders and requests; follow through with agents to maintain timely status of work; recordkeeping and report preparation.
Marketing:	Train, coordinate, and motivate staff personnel; deal with legal department regarding marketing problems or advertising/promotional matters; make continual evaluations of progress toward corporate goals. Introduce Medco programs and services to prospective clients; develop and maintain rapport with insurance agency managers and agents; participate in developing new marketing plans and objectives.
Public Relations:	Involved with local and national association life underwriters; assist home office in obtaining approval to service new insurance companies.
Medical:	Perform inspections of medical offices in the field; keep equipment maintained and insure that medical information is accurate; keep all supplies readily available for examiners. *January 1990 to December 1991* **DEPARTMENT SUPERVISOR** **Boston Memorial Hospital** Responsible for all procedures performed in Phlebotomy Department, including personnel and assignments.
Education	B.S., Marketing, Boston College, 1990.
References	References and other details furnished upon request

Original

Jerry Lowell Nash 205 Mason Drive, Apt. #42 Telephone:
Atlanta, Georgia 30341 404-322-6626

Job Objective: I am seeking a position in the Loss Prevention or
Security field that will offer an immediate
opportunity for advancement and job security.

Work Experience:
The Adolphus Hotel: 2114 Commerce Street, Atlanta, Georgia 30332
Security Officer, March 1992 to Present

Picadilly Gift Shop: 400 N. Olive, Atlanta, Georgia 30331
Manager, oversee entire store operations with a
staff of six cashiers, November 1991 to Present

The Westin Hotel: 13340 Greenville Parkway, Atlanta, Georgia
30349
Senior Officer, December 1990 to August 1985.

The Westin Peachtree 210 Peachtree Street, Atlanta, Georgia 30345
Plaza Hotel: Acting Shift Supervisor, Security Officer, Radio
Dispatcher, March 1988 to November 1990

C&G Services 1483 Avenue M College Park, Georgia
Collection Agency: Collector, August 1986 to May 1987

Bryan Street 349 Bryan Street, Atlanta, Georgia 44502,
Y.M.C.A: Resident Manager, March 1985 to August 1986.

Williams West 106 Chestnut Street, Atlanta, Georgia
Gateway Supermarket: Assistant Manager in charge of purchasing and
loss prevention, August 1983 to March 1985

Education

Western Kentucky University, Bowling Green, Kentucky
September, 1975 to December 1976, Major communication,
Minor in Psychology and Recreation
Flaget High School, Louisville, Kentucky
Diploma in Business
Atlanta Area Technical School, Atlanta, Georgia
Diploma in Private Investigation

Revised

Jerry Lowell Nash   205 Mason Drive #42   Telephone:
Atlanta, Georgia 30341   404-322-6626

POSITION
DESIRED

Seeking a position in SECURITY or LOSS PREVENTION where professional advancement and job security are based on performance.

WORK EXPERIENCE

THE
ADOLPHUS
HOTEL

Joined Atlanta's prestigious hotel in 11/91 as manager of the Picadilly Gift Shop, with responsibility for six employees and all of the retail sales operations.

Concurrent responsibilities (since 3/92) as a security officer include all routine security and loss prevention duties.

THE WESTIN
HOTEL

Began working for the Westin Corporation in 3/88 as security officer and acting radio dispatcher/shift supervisor at the newly built **Westin Peachtree Plaza Hotel.**

Transferred to **The Westin Hotel** in 12/84 as senior security officer in charge of implementing corporate security policies and procedures.

FORMAL
EDUCATION

Diploma in Private Investigation, 1987. Atlanta Area Technical School.

Coursework in communications and psychology. Western Kentucky University at Bowling Green.

Completed vocational/business program, 1985. Flaget High School, Louisville, Kentucky.

OTHER
EXPERIENCE

C&G Services Collection Agency, 1986–1987. Collector Bryan Street Y.M.C.A., 1985–1986. Resident Manager Various other jobs during high school, summer and vacations, and during college.

REFERENCES & LETTERS OF RECOMMENDATION AVAILABLE

PART FIVE

LETTERS

GUIDE TO LETTERS & CROSS-REFERENCE

Response to Advertisement: Same Title
See Resume on Page 111

4200 Hyannis Drive
Richmond, Virginia 23235

March 14, 1992

Mr. Robert Straszak
Manager, Field Services
REMORE COMPUTER SYSTEMS, INC.
404 Normandy
Columbus, Ohio

Dear Mr. Straszak:

Your recent advertisement for a field engineer in **Computer World** is of interest to me. I would like to know more about this opportunity, as I now have seven years of field service experience.

As a field engineer and computer specialist for my present employer (see attached resume), I have functioned with a wide latitude of independence while my territory has continued to be expanded by corporate headquarters.

Although my salary has increased along with my responsibilities, I believe I would be happier with a smaller geographical range and a more saturated customer base.

From my reading of technical journals and my conversations with associates and customers in the industry, I am aware of Remore's reputation for first-quality field engineering. I know this critical area well, both technically and with regard to customer relations, and I believe I would be an effective engineer and representative for Remore.

As indicated on my resume, I worked in the Columbus area for more than a year (1989–1990), and I would be pleased to return to that area. I could arrange to meet you in Columbus for a personal interview if you would like. A week's notice should be sufficient to work out a schedule.

I look forward to hearing from you in the near future.

Sincerely,

John Loughlin

Home: (804) 393-4502
Work: (804) 344-8255
Resume Enclosed

Response to Advertisement: Same Field, New Title
See Resume on Page 112

12 Mescal Court
Tucson, Arizona 85718
(602) 385-9932

22 February 1992

Ms. Maria Berriozabal
Aztec Management Services, Inc.
220 Winding Lane
Phoenix, Arizona

Dear Ms. Berriozabal,

Re your classified advertisement for a "versatile and highly experienced project manager" in the Tuscon Times (2-20-92), I am hereby submitting my resume for your consideration.

As you can see, I am currently working in Phoenix for Tri-State Properties. Prior to my transfer here I was managing their properties in Tucson. (My mother lives in a home I own there, and she can take messages; I can also be reached in Phoenix through my service: 499-8265.)

My property management background since 1985 has demanded considerable skills in financial planning/controls, marketing, contract negotiations, and the usual day-to-day problem solving that is so much a part of this type of work.

My experience with Majestic Realty in Austin, Texas (new construction) and with Barclay Management Company in Phoenix (renovation program management) is especially relevant to the qualifications you seek. I would enjoy discussing these with you in a personal interview.

In addition, my experience as project coordinator for Northern Telecom for four years might be of particular interest to you. I also know the local market quite well, and I am up to date on the zoning and housing ordinances of the Phoenix City Council.

I hope we may meet soon to discuss Aztec's plans and how I may be of benefit to your organization. Thank you.

Respectfully,

Minerva Vasquez

Resume Attached

Response to Advertisement: Switching Fields
See Resume on Page 109

See Resume on Page 109

4 Park Hill Drive
Apartment #235
Des Moines, Iowa 50312

March 5, 1992

Mr. Jerry Barton
National Sales Manager
Key Equipment Company
15 Broad Street
Webster City, Iowa

RE: SALES REPRESENTATIVE

Dear Mr. Barton:

Your advertisement in WAREHOUSING TODAY (Feb. 24th) stated that you are looking for "aggressive and motivated" sales representatives who know how to "get past the doors and to the buyers."

I can do that! With my combined experience as a buyer and user of warehouse equipment, I know what works and what doesn't. I can tell you how long it will take to train someone to operate a particular machine, and I can tell you how much to expect in downtime for most warehousing and inventory systems.

To me, selling a product is also selling an idea: The real bottom line of a Key product is the time ($$$) saved, as well as the substantial benefits derived from Key's safety features.

I've been on the inside watching the salesmen line up to show their goods. I know Key and I know your competitors. I'd like to show you what I can do.

If Key Equipment Company is willing to give me a ground-floor opportunity to demonstrate my motivation, I'm willing to give 100% effort to producing top-level profits. I am college educated and experienced in business.

I will call your office next week to see if we can set up an appointment. Meanwhile, my resume is enclosed.

Sincerely,

Susan Jane Hemingway

Resume (Enclosed)

Targeted: Local Query, Blind
See Resume on Page 110

699 Gainsboro Avenue
Detroit, Michigan 48220

18 March 1992

Lynette Bryan
Program Director
MICHCON
444 West End Avenue
Detroit, Michigan

Dear Ms. Bryan:

I am writing to you with the hope that you might have an opening soon in your organization. If you don't, I would very much appreciate your keeping my resume (enclosed) on file for future opportunities.

My experience with the Michigan Department of Human Resources (MDHR) has been extremely challenging and equally rewarding; in fact, I have learned more in the past six months than I had imagined possible.

However, as you probably know from the local media, MDHR is experiencing drastic budget cuts, and I have recently learned that my position will probably be eliminated within a few months.

I believe my caseload has been unusually heavy, requiring a lot of overtime and travel, but I am assured by my immediate superiors that I have done a good job in handling it. They have volunteered to attest to my professional conduct and reliability, and are as displeased as I am that we cannot continue our work together.

As noted on my resume, I am especially interested in the areas of marketing and public relations. I think I could do a good job of "selling the public" on the value and impact of MICHCON's diversified services. I have some ideas I would like to discuss with you when you have time. Please let me know when we may meet at your convenience.

Sincerely,

Kathy Ann Alsobrook

Office: 448-2232 Ext. 188

Targeted: Local Query, Contacted First
See Resume on Page 118

77 Ridgeway Lane #211
Denver, Colorado 60233

26 March 1992

Mr. Marvin Johnson
Manager, Computer Operations
SKI-BEV CORPORATION
10 Valley View
Denver, Colorado

Re: Programming/Production Support

Dear Mr. Johnson:

Last week I called your office and talked with your secretary (Jo-Ann), and she was kind enough to suggest I send you my resume (enclosed) and a brief letter.

Although she was not able to pin down the date of your conversion from Honeywell to IBM operations, she felt it would be within a month or less.

The bulk of my six years in computer operations has been IBM. More important, I have held a full spectrum of product support roles—scheduling, backup, vendor specification specialist—and I could easily adapt and train for other related positions.

I've operated IBM 3084 MVS/XA & 3081 MVS/XA & 3380. I know the idiosyncracies of the 3800 too. (You can expect some problems with the 3203 during the initial phase-in stages. A heat cover may correct it.)

My bachelor's degree is in data processing, and I have had special training in JCL and other areas. And I'm ready to make a move for more challenging activities.

Jo-Ann thought you might be looking quietly for an experienced (yet patient and resourceful) "right-hand person" to help put your staff "on line" with new procedures and backlogged job batches.

I can help you meet your objectives, short- and long-term. If you would like to speak with me in person, please contact me at home or office. I can work either day or night.

Sincerely,

Letitia Honowantine

Targeted: Regional, Limited Relocate
See Resume on Page 113

217 Sequoia Road NW
Albuquerque, New Mexico 87120

10 March 92

Mr. Edward Scott
General Manager
Office-Go Enterprises
244 Yucca Drive
Tucson, Arizona

Dear Mr. Scott:

Your personnel office directed me to contact you about any vacancies in managing your transportation operations.

Thus, my enclosed resume will show ten years of work experience in the business. Beyond my lengthy experience is the capacity to grow in a position.

I'm planning on moving to Tucson soon, and I would like to hear about any potential position with Office-Go.

Alcron, my present employer, is aware of my plans. I also have a letter from them that compliments me on my special achievements: reorganizing receiving/shipping departments, and starting a new safety/licensing program.

Here's a recap of other abilities and experience:

personnel: from supervisors to laborers

screening/hiring, evaluating/firing employees

scheduling, payroll, quality control

sales estimates, equipment maintenance, fleet leasing

I'm a "hands on" manager whose education came from the world of practicality. If I can manage with one truck or one crew, I make sure I don't have to pay for another one. If a worker is not cutting the mustard, I get rid of him. If I see a worker trying to improve, I reward him.

I'll be glad to provide more details if you wish. Let me know at my address above. I look forward to hearing from you.

Respectfully,

Robert (Bob) Hamilton

Enclosed: Resume

Targeted: National, Open
See Resume on Page 119

164-E Volvo Circuit Road
Bethesda, Maryland 20014

14 March 1992

Box 1888-A
Alamo Station Annex
San Antonio, Texas 78242

ATTN: HYDRAULICS ENGINEERING

Dear Sir/Madam:

The display ad in "Washington Engineering Works" newsletter (26 January) indicated you are now hiring. If this is true, please consider me an interested applicant.

The attached resume details my technical experience, eight years of installing, inspecting, and troubleshooting, as well as more provocative foreign assignments.

Parkan-Denton trained me in their "Four Step Service" program, and my firsthand experience with models PD 120, 100, 70, and 60 is extensive.

I am open to relocating anywhere—in the USA or internationally—and can begin full-time employment within a week's notice.

I look forward to your reply. Thanks.

Sincerely,

Michael B. Cottone

Call: 301-444-1963

Attachment: Resume
             WEW Newsletter

Targeted: Grapevine Contact
See Resume on Page 116

121 Mountain Valley Road
Portland, Oregon 97229

26 March 1992

Mrs. Dorothy Blake
Director of Sales
BROUSSARD PROFILES
2600 Carnes Boulevard
Seattle, Washington

Dear Mrs. Blake:

Karen Livingston, who works out of Broussard's Portland office, informed me that your company plans to set up new operations in Vancouver, British Columbia, next year.

Congratulations! I think it's about time the Canadians have access to top-shelf products.

Before I moved to Portland in 1985, and before I started a career in sales, I lived in Vancouver and worked as a market researcher in an important government-sponsored study of regional commerce and topical consumer patterns. It afforded the opportunity to foresee changes in economic and cultural changes.

My resume is enclosed, which outlines my employment history. However, I believe my truly valuable skills are incorporated within my personable style of managing people. My ability to resolve staff conflicts and client problems is also an asset.

Karen speaks very highly of Broussard's goals and leading executives, and having been one of your customers for a long time, I can agree with her.

Please take a look at my resume; talk with Karen if you like. I would love to become a part of your Vancouver sales team! I hope to hear from you very soon.

Very truly,

Annie Boyd

Copy: Karen Livingston
Enclosed: Resume

Targeted: A Probe
See Resume on Page 121

See Resume on Page 121

1600 High Line Drive
Birmingham, AL 35217

24 February 1992

Rita Carato
Public Relations Department
SPACE & LIGHT STORES
400 Thames Drive
Mobile, Alabama

Dear Rita:

Your recent appearance on KTTL-TV's "Corporate Moves" show was a pleasure to watch. It was good news to hear that your company plans to move its headquarters here in Birmingham.

I am a mature and seasoned secretary and administrative assistant, and I know Birmingham well because I have lived here most of my life. (My husband has been an architect here for twenty years.)

You mentioned on the show that you would be glad to hear from anyone interested in employment with your firm, so I am enclosing my resume.

Just as important as my skills and experience is my detailed knowledge of the city: post offices, traffic patterns, photocopying and courier services, and contacts with people at all levels in the residential and commercial building trades.

I enjoy secretarial work and have no aspirations to take on the added responsibilities of office manager or similar positions. If your company is searching for reliable and competent administrative support personnel, I have the qualifications.

Looking forward to your response and thanking you in advance for your consideration, I am,

Sincerely,

Delilah Grace Williams

Resume Enclosed

Student: Response to Advertisement
See Resume on Page 138

555 Hawthorne #34-A
Dallas, Texas 75211
(214) 383-3774

20 March 1992

Songbird Video Systems
2800 Loma Vista
Minneapolis, Minnesota

To Whom It May Concern

In four months I will be graduating with an associate of arts degree in video production and technology from Video Arts Technical College of Dallas.

My formal program has included fifty weeks of electronics technology and troubleshooting, and forty weeks of on-the-job training in production, including both video and audio.

My resume, enclosed, highlights my skills and lists the vast array of production (pre- and post-production included) equipment I have personally used in my training.

My primary objective is to start working in my profession, so I am flexible enough to accept whatever position might be available to start my career in this exciting field.

Although a current resident of Dallas, I plan to return to Minneapolis (my home town) as soon as I can. I hope you can take a minute from your busy schedule to let me know if you would like to discuss this in more detail.

Thank you.

Respectfully,

Bobby Reynolds

Resume Enclosed

Transcript Available: VATCD Placement Office

Student: Shotgun Strategy
See Resume on Page 139

See Resume on Page 139

149 Sunflower—L.A., CA 90035
213/484-1127

9 March 1992

Mr. J. R. Williams
Personnel Director
Wilson Research Hospital
1800 Crossing Cove
San Francisco, CA

Dear Mr. Williams:

I am interested in applying for a position at Wilson Research Hospital; thus, my curriculum vitae is attached.

My graduate degree (I have nine more hours to finish) will be in biochemistry; my undergraduate degree (1989) was in chemistry, and I graduated **summa cum laude.**

My experience as an EKG and laboratory technician has helped pay my college expenses while allowing me to learn through the workplace as well.

My technical knowledge of research methods, materials, and procedures is excellent, and I am accustomed to the demands of stringent quality controls.

If you are interested in knowing more please let me know. I can provide further information if you would like.

You may contact Miss Brandywine in the placement office (213-344-8711) if you would like to know more about the academic program(s).

Sincerely,

Evana Saroj

Military: Shotgun Strategy
See Resume on Page 144

359 East 50 Street #62
New York City 10013
Phone: (212) 432-8821

27 February 1992

Microwave Systems Division
PHILLIPS AIR-LINKS INC.
Box UX-777
Houston, Texas

RE: MICROWAVE REPAIR/TROUBLESHOOTING

Dear Sirs:

Please accept this letter and the attached resume as an application for employment with Phillips Air-Links.

Qualifications:

1—Six years of U.S. Army electronics experience.
2—Specialized direct support shop responsibilities.
3—Four years of technical training programs.
4—Hands-on experience with state-of-the-art systems.
5—Ability to perform well under pressure.

I will be available for interviews and employment as of the 20th of March. I can forward additional data if so desired. Copies of APR's and training certificates available upon request.

I look forward to hearing from you soon.

Sincerely,

Jesse Rodriquez

Resume Attached

Military: Response to Advertisement
See Resume on Page 146

A. J. Gresham
[Until 28 June 1986]
106 North White, Altus, OK 73422
(405) 724-6288

2 March 1992

Attn: David Bell
WORLDWAYS CARGO
Building RC-4, Box 99
Cincinnati, Ohio

Dear Mr. Bell:

This is in response to your 19 February classified advertisement as seen in Air World magazine.

My immediate job objective is to work as an aircraft maintenance mechanic. I will have six years of this experience when I get out of the Air Force in June, 1992. I also have an A&P license.

My background includes C-141B and C-5A aircraft: airframe component inspection and removal/repair, jacking, and determining what parts need to be ordered.

I believe my extensive training and firsthand experience, along with my attitude and performance (see "comments" on the enclosed resume), could be of benefit to your maintenance group.

I hope to hear from you soon. Please note that on the resume the permanent address (Fairfax, Virginia) should be used after June 20th. Thank you.

Respectfully,

Abraham Gresham

Resume Enclosed

Follow-up: Basic
See Resume on Page 115

41 Confederate Lane
Atlanta, Georgia 30341

27 March 1991

Mr. Daniel Kirby
TELE-KOMMIN
14 Cole Plaza
Philadelphia, Pennsylvania

Dear Dan,

It was certainly a pleasure meeting with you last Tuesday.

I'm sure that the person you are looking for is as important to you as your firm is to me. I'm aware of your needs at present and that I can fulfill them, but even more important, I believe I can be an asset for your future needs as well.

I'm attaching the resume you requested. Let me know if you would like more information, or a list of references in your area.

You can reach me at home on weekends (404-522-1990) or at my office (404-522-8821).

Best regards,

Johnny K. Madison

Follow-up: Recap
See Resume on Page 181

See Resume on Page 181

5624 West Trout   New Orleans, LA 70126

28 March 1992

Mr. Darin Kline
Drummer Corporation
222 Seaside Boulevard
San Francisco, California

Dear Mr. Kline:

Last night we talked over the phone about my interest in the Drummer Corporation. I would like the opportunity to interview with DC for a management-related position in your San Diego plant. I have admired your company for some time and I know I can contribute to its continued success.

The past three years I have been with General Dynamics in New Orleans working as an engineering section manager in the corporate services division. I enjoy the challenges and responsibilities of my position, but my wife and I have decided to relocate to the San Diego area. In making this move, I am also looking for the personal and professional growth that a company such as Drummer Corporation has to offer.

My tenure at GD has provided me with some excellent experience in engineering management and project coordination. My performance has been very good. The first year my performance rating was "2" (very good). The past two years I have received four ratings of "1" (outstanding). I have also received two major responsibility promotions and two job grade promotions.

I worked my way through school, receiving my MBA from Tulane University in 1992, and my BS in mechanical engineering from Gonzaga University in 1988.

I am exceptionally strong in the areas of interpersonal skills, communication, personal integrity, and acceptance of responsibility. I am serious about my interest in DC and want to make a dedicated commitment to my job there.

If you wish to contact me by phone, I am usually home after 6:30 PM (your time). You may call me at my office (504-335-2988) with a message, but I would not likely be able to talk in confidence, nor do I believe in using the company's time for my personal use.

I have enclosed my resume for your records. I would be able to start work at the end of May.

Sincerely,

L. Byron Shubert

Enclosure: Resume

Follow-up: Clarification
See Resume on Page 179

104 Walker Avenue
Arlington, Texas 76012
(817) 499-2388

25 March 1992

Ms. Sandy Greene
Executive Vice President
BRANDIE'S HOT GRILLES, INCORPORATED
2900 Northern Lights Circle
Chicago, Illinois

Dear Ms. Greene:

I enjoyed our brief meeting last week, and I have given considerable thought to what transpired.

Let me emphasize that my sole and singular objective is to put together the best possible marketing team for Brandie's. I have absolutely no desire to slip into the national sales manager's position.

With all my marketing experience in the food service industry, I feel I can make the most of my many contacts in the business: wholesalers and suppliers, personnel recruiters, advertising agencies.

As I told you, I have been in charge of strategy development for at least ten years now, and this is my true interest.

I'm an aggressive yet tactful producer. I want and expect results. I want to earn a good living by doing good work. My achievements are due to both my resourcefulness and my refusal to get bogged down by problems.

I'm prepared to prove my capabilities. I don't expect anyone just to take my word for it. My basic philosophy is "let me show you, not tell you." My track record stands up to it.

This is an exciting opportunity for me and I believe Brandie's has great potential. I'd like to be part of your winning team!

I hope this clears up any confusion concerning my motivation and goals. I would be glad to meet with you again to provide additional details.

Sincerely,

Bill Ridgestone

A Case Study: Letter # 1 (Accepts Job)

404 West Fork Road
Santa Fe, New Mexico 88288

10 March 1992

Mr. Raul Martinez
CopperLight Industries, Inc.
55 Wagon Wheel Circle
Albuquerque, New Mexico

Dear Raul,

I would like to express my appreciation to you for your time and interest with regard to the position of marketing coordinator for your Las Cruces facility.

The challenge of the opportunity is an exciting one, and I am confident I will be able to generate maximum sales volume for CopperLight Industries! I feel fortunate to be able to join an aggressive and growing company.

I thought you might like to have a brief background sketch of my education and experience. Here are the essentials:

College: Attended UNM from 1984–1988 on a 4-year academic scholarship; graduated with a B.S., Marketing. Member of Sigma Chi and American Marketing Association. Also participated in intramural football and track. Earned approximately 80% of college expenses.

Sales: Since May, 1991 I have been employed by National Metals, Inc., reporting directly to Mr. Charles Dodd, Executive V.P., 30 Elm Street, Santa Fe, NM 88285.

As a sales rep. I established the SW United States territory, comprised of Texas, New Mexico, and Nevada. My primary responsibility has been to develop new accounts by promoting recognition and approval by engineers of our upgraded specifications related to precast manholes and resilient connectors.

I have called directly on the concrete pipe and pre-cast industry to introduce and sell the "core-drilling" concept which gives the end-user (contractor) a finished, high-quality product.

Since I started developing my territory, I have been able to establish seven new major (profitable) accounts, as well as broaden general product recognition.

I hope this mini-resume will answer any questions regarding my experience and abilities. Thanks again, Raul, and I hope we can make CopperLight's Santa Fe operation a leader!

Sincerely,

Chris Cooper

Home: 505/255-5507

A Case Study: Letter #2 (Changes Mind)

404 West Fork Road
Santa Fe, New Mexico 88288

20 March 1992

Mr. Raul Martinez
CopperLight Industries, Inc.
55 Wagon Wheel Circle
Albuquerque, New Mexico

Dear Raul,

I would like to take this opportunity to express my sincere appreciation for your time and consideration in offering me a position with CopperLight Industries.

I know CopperLight is a first-class company and that you are a determined and well-liked leader, and I'm sure you will put together a successful team that will do a great job.

If my strong initial response to your offer has created any difficulties for you, please accept my apologies, as I am fully aware of how valuable your time is. I know that you have been in the industry long enough to understand the predicaments one can get into when career decisions must be made.

National Metals has made an offer I can't refuse: new products to sell in an expanded territory, and a greatly improved financial package to go with it. Thus, having spent a year with them already, I cannot help but feel that another year or more would reap substantial benefits in both professional growth and financial security.

I look forward to our continuing business association and the opportunity to provide CopperLight Industries with the best products in the industry. I hope you understand that I have a personal interest in helping you and your staff make CopperLight an industry leader.

Again, I regret causing you any trouble if that is the case. Please let me know if I can be of any assistance.

Sincerely,

Chris Cooper

A Case Study: Letter #3 (Covers Tracks)

404 West Fork Road
Santa Fe, New Mexico 88288

24 March 1992

Mr. Charles Dodd
Executive V.P., Sales
National Metals, Incorporated
30 Elm Street
Santa Fe, New Mexico

Dear Charlie:

I would like to take this opportunity to clear up any doubts or confusion concerning my professional interests in CopperLight Industries.

During my numerous meetings with Mr. Raul Martinez he indicated that CLI was looking for a qualified candidate for coordinating their new Las Cruces marketing activities. It was a challenging position and when he approached me later with an invitation to take on the job, I was simply caught off guard.

I gave considerable thought to the ramifications of such a change: a solid offer, professionally demanding role, and certainly less travel. The pressure was on and my career seemed to depend on the decision I made.

However, with the new product lines NMI is going to be offering Copper-Light and others, and the improved salary and commission structure NMI has offered, I concluded it would be wise to continue building my success with NMI, having already invested an important year of my professional development.

CopperLight is a good client and I believe I have dealt with Mr. Martinez in a professional manner and will continue to maintain a good, productive rapport with him and his staff. I know he understands my situation and will develop into one of my best customers because he realizes I have a particular interest in helping his company now.

Let me assure you that I intend to give NMI my best efforts, and I am determined to produce 100%. I am enclosing a copy of my letter to Mr. Martinez so you can see how I am dealing with this situation—a new one for me.

My regards,

Chris Cooper

Copy: Letter to CLI (3-20-92)

APPENDIX

1. KEY TELEGRAPHIC TERMINOLOGY

A
act as
active in
administer
allocate
analyze
approve
articulate
assimilate
assist
assure
augment

B
balance
bring about

C
collect
communicate
compute
conceptualize
consolidate
consult
contribute
control
coordinate
correct
correspond
counsel
create

D
demonstrate
design
determine
develop
direct
distribute

document
draft

E
effect
enact
establish
evaluate
examine
execute

F
follow up
forecast
formulate
forward to

G
generate
guide

I
identify
implement
inform
initiate
install
institute
integrate
interface
interview

L
launch
liaison
locate

M
maintain
manage
monitor

O
optimize
orchestrate
organize
oversee

P
plan
prepare
present
process
produce

project
promote
propose
provide
purchase

R
receive
recommend
recruit
report
represent

research
resolve
respond to
review
revise

S
schedule
screen
secure
select
set up

spearhead
supervise
supply

T
test
train

U
update
upgrade
utilize

2. WORKSHEETS

First Name	Middle or Nickname	Last Name

Street Address	Apartment Number

City	State	Zip Code

Home Phone	Business Phone	Messages/Service

CAREER/JOB OBJECTIVES

Immediate Goal

_____
_____
_____

Long-term Goal

_____
_____
_____

Willing to Travel? Restrictions? _____

Willing to Relocate? Geographical Preference? _____
_____

QUALIFICATIONS SUMMARY

Primary Skills
_____
_____
_____

Specific Experience
_____
_____
_____

Special Skills
_____
_____
_____

Special Experience
_____
_____
_____

FORMAL EDUCATION

Graduate Degree _____
College _____
Dates Attended _____

Major/Concentration

_____
_____
_____

Honors/Awards

_____
_____
_____

Membership/Activities

_____
_____
_____

Undergraduate Degree _____
College _____
Dates Attended _____
Major _____ *Hours* _____
Honors/Awards _____
Extracurricular Activities _____

EMPLOYMENT HISTORY

Present/Most Recent Employer

_____
_____
_____

Dates _____ *to* _____
City & State _____
Title _____

Major Responsibilities

_____

_____

_____

Major Contributions

_____

_____

_____

Previous Positions & Dates

_____

_____

_____

Dates _____ to _____
Company _____
City & State _____
Title _____
Primary Responsibilities & Achievements

_____

_____

_____

Dates _____ to _____
Company _____
City & State _____
Title _____
Primary Responsibilities & Achievements

_____

_____

_____

Dates _____ *to* _____
Company _____
City & State _____
Title _____
Primary Responsibilities & Achievements

_____
_____
_____

Dates _____ *to* _____
Company _____
City & State _____
Title _____
Primary Responsibilities & Achievements

_____
_____
_____

Dates _____ *to* _____
Company _____
City & State _____
Title _____
Primary Responsibilities & Achievements

_____
_____
_____

Dates _____ *to* _____
Company _____
City & State _____
Title _____

Primary Responsibilities & Achievements

_____
_____
_____

SPECIAL TRAINING

Seminars/Workshops

_____
_____
_____

Technical Training

_____
_____
_____

RELATED SKILLS & EXPERIENCE

Languages _____
Skills & Equipment

_____
_____
_____

Travel _____
Publications

_____
_____
_____

Membership/Activities

_____
_____
_____

Military Service

_____
_____
_____

BIODATA

Date of Birth _____ *Marital Status* _____

Hobbies & Interests _____

NOTES

NOTES

NOTES

NOTES

NOTES